KU-570-537

Penguin Handbooks
Leaves from our Tuscan Kitchen

Janet Duff Gordon, later Janet Ross, was born in 1842,
the daughter of the Lady Duff Gordon who wrote the
celebrated *Letters from Egypt*, and the grand-daughter of
John Austin, the jurist. Her youth was spent in a literary
circle. (She was the Rose Jocelyn of Meredith's *Evan
Harrington*.) On her marriage to Henry Ross, who had
helped Henry Layard with his excavations at Nimrud, she
and her husband settled in Tuscany, in a fascinating
Trecento Italian villa, Poggio Gherardo, just outside
Florence. Giuseppe Volpi, who was her cook for thirty
years, together with his successors, established a tradition
of good cooking there. The recipes were carefully
recorded by Mrs Ross and first published in the original
edition of *Leaves from our Tuscan Kitchen* in 1899. Janet Ross
died in 1927.

Michael Waterfield is Janet Ross's great-great-nephew,
himself a cook of renown and a restaurateur, and the
owner of the Wife of Bath Restaurant at Wye in Kent.

Janet Ross and Michael Waterfield

Leaves from our Tuscan Kitchen

or how to cook vegetables

Line drawings by
Michael Waterfield

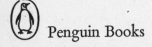 Penguin Books

Penguin Books Ltd,
Harmondsworth Middlesex, England
Penguin Books,
625 Madison Avenue, New York, New York 10022, U.S.A.
Penguin Books Australia Ltd,
Ringwood, Victoria, Australia
Penguin Books Canada Ltd, 2801 John Street,
Markham, Ontario, Canada L3R 1B4
Penguin Books (N.Z.) Ltd,
182–190 Wairau Road, Auckland 10, New Zealand

First published 1899
This edition first published by John Murray 1973
Published in Penguin Handbooks 1977
Reprinted 1978

This edition copyright © Michael Waterfield, 1973
All rights reserved

Made and printed in Great Britain by
Cox & Wyman Ltd,
London, Reading and Fakenham
Set in Monotype Bembo

Except in the United States of America, this
book is sold subject to the condition that
it shall not, by way of trade or otherwise, be lent,
re-sold, hired out, or otherwise circulated without
the publisher's prior consent in any form of
binding or cover other than that in which it is
published and without a similar condition
including this condition being imposed on the
subsequent purchaser

Contents

Introductory Note

The first edition of this book was published in 1899 by J. M. Dent, and its last, the eleventh, in 1936. Nearly forty years have intervened and copies have become rare, but when found are among the treasured possessions in gourmets' households. There is today a growing interest in good cooking, a change from the end of last century, when Janet Ross wrote:

> Not so very long ago soup was an exception in English houses – almost a luxury. A dish of vegetables – as a dish and not an adjunct to meat – was a still greater rarity; and even now plain-boiled potatoes, peas, cabbages, etc. are the rule ...
>
> For years English friends have begged recipes for cooking vegetables in the Italian fashion, so I have written down many of the following from the dictation of our good Giuseppe Volpi ... who has been known to our friends for over thirty years ...

Giuseppe was undoubtedly a very fine cook, as were his successors Agostino Sabattini and Carlo Guerrini, for many years a well-known chef in a London City bank. Maria Chiodetti, who still cooks for the family at the Castello della Brunella at Aulla, worked for some time in the kitchen at Poggio Gherardo, there acquiring the tradition of good cooking. Her vegetable dishes are specially appreciated by visitors who stay at the Castle. Janet Ross took great trouble in setting down the recipes from her chefs, to which she added others later. I found, however, in editing the recipes and using most of them in my restaurant, that there were some weights and measures which had to be corrected.

In editing these recipes I have omitted some elaborate dishes. Truffles in champagne, for example, which seems to have been dear to the Edwardians, and delicacies which were remote in their aspic are now also remote in their appeal; but the form of the original book remains basically unchanged.

The vegetables are placed alphabetically for immediate reference, with mixed vegetables, salads, rice and spaghetti dishes and soups taking their place at the end. Cross-reference should not be necessary, as each recipe is complete with its own sauce or manner of serving. All the recipes are for six people.

The lay-out of the recipes has been altered from Janet Ross's narrative form to one where ingredients and method are combined side by side, which should be easier to follow. Oven temperatures and a metric conversion table appear before the recipes.

I had always been interested in my great-great-aunt Janet, having heard about her adventurous life from my family, but it was not until I met the late Sir Harry Luke, who was himself a gourmet and the author of a fine cookery book, that I realized how well-known her book had become in its time. When it was decided to publish a new edition he was kind enough to say that he would like to write about the book and Janet Ross as a Foreword and, to my great pleasure, that is what he did.

The Wife of Bath,   MICHAEL WATERFIELD
Wye, Kent

Foreword

Leaves from our Tuscan Kitchen is the first cookery book I ever possessed; I made its acquaintance on one of the Tuscan holidays of my teenage youth at the same time as I made that of the authoress herself. In the sixty-six years that have elapsed since then I must have earned the gratitude of scores of my women friends through introducing them, by means of this precious little volume – a blessing to him that gives no less than to her that takes – to the delights of the best Italian home cooking.

When Janet Ross's *Leaves* made their appearance in the ante-penultimate year of Queen Victoria, Mrs Beeton's monumental work of over a thousand pages still deservedly dominated the English kitchen, perhaps admitting from 1920 onwards, in the houses of the more discerning eaters and drinkers, the juxtaposition of Professor George Saintsbury's slender classic, *Notes on a Cellar-Book*, but of little else. The stream of the delightful cookery books – decorative, readable, practical – that nowadays fill shelf upon shelf of the gourmet's library was then little more than a trickle, let alone coursing in full spate. Mrs Ross's bantling was, so far as this country was concerned, something of a pioneer. Even in France, so infinitely more food-conscious than the British Isles, Brillat-Savarin, although sprung from an earlier century than Mrs Beeton, was still the Frenchman's and Frenchwoman's unquestioned oracle on culinary taste and etiquette.

It says much for the intrinsic merit of Mrs Ross's unassuming little book, now entering upon its seventh decade, that it should have achieved a viability in the literature of gastronomy hitherto attained only by the giants. But quite a number of contributory causes may explain this phenomenon. An obvious one is the perennial appeal of Italy to the peoples of the British Isles – an appeal promoted by the English humanists of the Renaissance; powerfully stimulated by the nobility and gentry of the eighteenth and early nineteenth centuries, who lumbered south in their coaches on the Grand Tour to return with acres of paintings and tons of statuary for the stocking of their Palladian mansions; and since then maintained by the innumerable travellers of all ages and classes who delight to follow less pompously in their trail.

Another reason is the British people's growing interest in intelligent eating already referred to. A third, surely, is the fact that Janet Ross's recipes were those actually in use in her beloved Poggio Gherardo, that fascinating Trecento villa (in the Italian sense of 'villa') outside Florence with its echoes of Boccaccio and the telling of the tales of the Decameron. And then there is the personality of the authoress herself.

Janet Duff Gordon, afterwards Janet Ross, was born in 1842 and died in 1927; she was the daughter of the Lady Duff Gordon who wrote the celebrated *Letters from Egypt* and grand-daughter of John Austin, the jurist. Her youth was spent in a literary circle, and she is the Rose Jocelyn of Meredith's *Evan Harrington*. On her marriage to Henry Ross, a man more than twenty years her senior who had helped Henry Layard with his excavations at Nimrud, she and her husband settled in Tuscany, where she came to be regarded by some of her contemporaries as a somewhat formidable person. Even as a child she had been unusually strong-minded and she once refused a request to tie Tennyson's shoe-lace. She could certainly be alarming if roused, with her determined jaw, white hair and beetling black brows; her feud with Ouida has passed into the social history of the nineteenth-century Florence, and somewhat one-sidedly, into Ouida's *roman à clef*, *Friendship*. Yet she could be approachable by the young, as I, at least, found her to be.

For all too long, however, the *Leaves* have been out of print; and it is with a nice appropriateness that this new and long-awaited reissue should be edited by Janet Ross's great-great-nephew, by profession a restaurateur. She, who produced at Poggio Gherardo not only books but a rather special vermouth, will appreciate that partnership from the Elysian fields.

HARRY LUKE

Preface to the Original Edition

The innate love of change in man is visible even in the kitchen. Not so very long ago soup was an exception in English houses – almost a luxury. A dish of vegetables – as a dish and not an adjunct to meat – was a still greater rarity; and even now plain-boiled potatoes, peas, cabbages, etc. are the rule. When we read of the dishes, fearfully and wonderfully made, in the old Italian *novelle*, we wonder whence the present Italians got their love of vegetables and maccheroni.

Sacchetti tells us that in the fourteenth century a baked goose, stuffed with garlic and quinces, was considered an exquisite dish; and when the gonfalonier of Florence gave a supper to a famous doctor, he put before him the stomach of a calf, boiled partridges, and pickled sardines. Gianfigliazzi's cook sent up a roasted crane to his master as a delicacy, says Boccaccio; and a dish of leeks cooked with spices appears as a special dish in the rules of the chapter of San Lorenzo when the canons messed together. Old Laschi, author of that delightful book *L'Osservatore Fiorentino*, moralizes on the ancient fashion of cooking in his pleasant rather prosy way:

It would not seem that the senses should be subjected to fashion; and yet such is the case. The perfumes, once so pleasing, musk, amber, and benzoin, now excite convulsions; sweet wines, such as Pisciancio, Verdea, Montalcino, and others mentioned by Redi in his dithyrambic, are now despised; and instead of the heavy dishes of olden times, light and elegant ones are in vogue. Whoever characterized man as a laughing animal ought rather to have called him a variable and inconstant one.

The dinner which set all Siena laughing for days, given to a favourite of Pius II by a Sienese who substituted wild geese for peacocks, after cutting off their beaks and feet, and coloured his jelly with poisonous ingredients, forms the subject of one of Pulci's tales:

Meanwhile it was ordered that hands should be washed, and Messer Goro was seated at the head of the table, and then other courtiers who had accompanied him; and they ate many tarts of good almond paste as a beginning. Then was brought to Messer Goro the dish on which were the peacocks without beaks, and a fellow was told to carve them. He not being used to such office gave himself vast trouble to pluck them,* but did it with so little grace that he filled the room and all the table with feathers, and the eyes, the mouth, the nose, and the ears of Messer Goro, and of them all. They, perceiving that it was from want of knowledge, held their peace, and took a mouthful here and there of other dishes so as not to disturb the order of the feast. But they were always swallowing dry feathers. Falcons and hawks would have been convenient that evening. When this pest had been removed many other roasts were brought, but all most highly seasoned with cumin. Everything would, however, have been pardoned if at the last an error had not been committed, which out of sheer folly nearly cost Messer Goro and those with him their lives. Now you must know that the master of the house and his councillors, in order to do honour to his guest, had ordered a dish of jelly. They wanted, as is the fashion in Florence and elsewhere, to have the arms of the Pope and of Messer Goro with many ornaments on it; so they used orpiment, white and red lead, verdigris and other horrors, and set this before Messer Goro as a choice and new thing. And Messer Goro and his companions ate willingly of it to take the bitter taste of the cumin and the other strange dishes out of their mouths, thinking, as is the custom in every decent place, that they were all coloured with saffron, milk of sweet almonds, the juices of herbs, and such like. And in the night it was just touch and go that some of them did not stretch out their legs. Messer Goro especially suffered much anguish from both head and stomach . . .

A company of Lombard pastrycooks came to Tuscany in the sixteenth century, and introduced fine pastry into Florence. We find the first mention of it in Berni's *Orlando Innamorato*, where it is mentioned among the choice viands. Laschi says 'the epoch of Charles V is the greatest of modern times, for the culture of the spirit induced the culture of the body'. But he does not mention vegetables or herbs at all. For them we must go back to the ancients. Bitterly did the Israelites, when wandering in the desert, regret 'the cucumbers and the melons we did eat in Egypt'; though old Gerarde says 'they yield to the body a cold and moist nourishment, and that very little, and the same not good'. Gerarde is, however, hard to please, for he says of egg-plants, under the old English name of Raging or Mad Apples, 'doubtless these apples have a mischievous qualitie, the use whereof is utterly to be forsaken'.

Fennel, dedicated to St John, was believed to make the lean fat and to

---

* Peacocks were skinned, not plucked, before cooking, and the skin with the feathers was put on to the roasted bird, and the tail opened out before placing the dish on the table. The 'fellow' ought to have cut the stitches and drawn off the skin, instead of plucking the feathers.

give the weak strength, while the root pounded with honey was considered a remedy against the bites of mad dogs. If lettuce be eaten after dinner it cures drunkenness; but Pope says:

> If your wish be rest,
> Lettuce and cowslip wine, *probatum est.*

Sorrel is under the influence of Venus, and Gerarde declares that also 'the carrot serveth for love matters; and Orpheus, as Pliny writeth, said that the use hereof winneth love'. Flowers of rosemary, rue, sage, marjoram, fennel, and quince preserve youth; worn over the heart they give gaiety. Rosemary is an herb of the sun, while Venus first raised sweet marjoram, therefore young married couples are crowned with it in Greece. While

> He that eats sage in May
> Shall live for aye.

Sweet basil is often worn by the Italian maidens in their bosoms, as it is supposed to engender sympathy, and borage makes men merry and joyful.

JANET ROSS

Conversion tables

Oven temperature

Cool and very cool	200°F–300°F	$\frac{1}{4}$–2 regulo setting
Moderate	300°F–375°F	2–5 regulo setting
Moderate to hot	375°F–400°F	6 regulo setting
Hot	400°F–475°F	6–9 regulo setting

Liquid measures

1 litre = $1\frac{3}{4}$ pints
2 pts approx. 1·15 litres
1 pt approx. 0·57 litre
$\frac{1}{2}$ pt approx. 0·28 litre
$\frac{1}{4}$ pt approx. 0·14 litre

Weights

1 kilo = 2 lb. 3 oz.
1 oz. approx. 28 g
2 oz. approx. 56 g
3 oz. approx. 84 g
4 oz. approx. 112 g
5 oz. approx. 142 g
6 oz. approx. 170 g
8 oz. approx. 227 g
12 oz. approx. 340 g
1 lb. approx. 453 g
$1\frac{1}{2}$ lb. approx. 686 g
2 lb. approx. 906 g

Globe Artichokes/*Carciofi*

The globe artichoke is bred from the cardoon. In Italy there are two main types, the Moretti, which are small, and the Romani, which are large and spiny.

They are eaten on the continent when half grown, the reason being that the leaves are more tender and the choke has not developed. In Italy the season is winter and spring. In England the most usual type grown is the larger spiny artichoke, but far superior is the Gros Vert de Laon, which is small and can be eaten whole.

The usual care must be taken in buying artichokes, that they are young and fresh and that they have not developed too much choke. They quickly lose their juice once they have been cut, which toughens the fibres in the leaves.

1   Carciofi bolliti

Boiled artichokes; hot with Hollandaise sauce or cold with a special dressing

Cut off the stalks, pull off the outer leaves and trim the bases of

six large artichokes.

Cut off, too, the top third of the artichoke, which is inedible. Put them into plenty of

boiling salted water –

the base of the artichoke downwards. Cook for about twenty minutes or until the base is soft to the point of a small knife. If over-cooked they will lose their nutty flavour. Remove and drain well if they are to be served hot; or refresh in cold water and then drain if to be served cold. Once cooked they will not keep more than a day.

If they are being served hot, prepare the following Hollandaise sauce while the artichokes are cooking:

Melt, but do not over-heat

6 oz. butter.

Beat over hot water
together with
and

*4 egg yolks
juice of ½ a lemon
a small pinch of basil.*

Beat the egg yolks and lemon until creamy and thickening. Then remove from the hot water and stir in the butter slowly and thoroughly. If it is

not as thick as thick cream, return to
the hot water and beat a while longer.

Serve the artichokes on a napkin
surrounding a pot of the sauce.

If they are to be served cold, prepare
the following vinaigrette, taking
care to use the best olive oil.

In a basin put	*a pinch of salt and pepper*
	a pinch of chopped marjoram
	and a teaspoon of French
	mustard.
Stir in	*2 tablespoons wine vinegar*
and then	*6 tablespoons olive oil.*

Mix well.

Serve the artichokes on a bed of
lettuce surrounding a pot of the sauce.
If fresh marjoram is available, put a
small sprig in the top of each
artichoke.

2 Carciofi alla Francese

Small peeled artichokes boiled in water and oil and finished with lemon

Here is one of the finest ways of eating artichokes.

Trim the bases and cut off almost half the tops of *twelve young small artichokes.*

Pull off about three layers of the leaves until only the light green tender ones are left. Cut them into quarters, putting them into a basin of cold water as they are prepared. Then put them into an open pan, barely covered with *boiling water with 6 tablespoons of good olive oil salt and twelve roughly crushed peppercorns.*

Boil until the water has evaporated and add the *juice of a lemon.*

Serve hot or cold with a sprinkling of chopped parsley.

3   Carciofi all'Italiana

Hot, boiled artichokes with a cold sauce Tartare

Trim the bases and the tops of

six large artichokes.

Boil them in salted water for about twenty minutes or until the point of a knife sinks into the base. Drain and serve at once on a napkin with the following sauce:

Chop very, very finely or liquidize

2 anchovies
a small onion or shallot
3 sprigs of tarragon
a tablespoon of capers.

Then add
and mix in

1 tablespoon wine vinegar
2 egg yolks.

Finally blend in until it thickens,
like a mayonnaise,

6 tablespoons olive oil.

4   Carciofi alla panna

Small artichokes cooked in stock which is reduced, finished with cream and lemon juice

Trim the bases and cut off almost half the top of

twelve young artichokes.

Pull off the outer leaves until only the tender light green ones are left. Put the artichokes into cold water as they are prepared.

Put them into an open pan, barely cover them with stock, add a little salt and pepper and boil fast until the stock has all but gone. Shake in

¼ pint of cream.

Let it bubble and thicken a moment on the stove. Remove the pan from the stove and stir in

the juice of a lemon.

Serve in little pots with chopped parsley.

5 Carciofi fritti

Small artichokes, dipped in light batter and deep-fried, served with lemon or tomato and garlic sauce

Trim the bases and cut off one third of the tops of

twelve young artichokes.

Pull off the outer leaves and cut across into about four slices, putting them into a basin of cold water as you do them.

Make the following batter, with

2 heaped tablespoons flour.

Form a well, add
and

1 egg yolk
1 tablespoon olive oil
pepper and salt.

Mix and start stirring in the flour, adding about
until the batter is like thick cream.

½ cup water

Let it rest while you beat up the

white of one egg.

Fold this into the batter.
Heat two or three inches of oil in a deep pan until it begins to smoke. Dip the pieces of artichoke into the batter, drain for a moment and fry in the oil until golden.

Serve with quarters of lemon or the following sauce:

Grate
into a pan with

½ an onion
2 tablespoons olive oil.

Add	*a good pinch chopped basil*
	parsley
and	*1 crushed clove of garlic.*
Stew for a few minutes then stir in	*twelve sliced tomatoes (or a tin).*
Season with	*salt and pepper*
and boil until creamy.	

---

6 Carciofi farciti

Small artichokes boiled, stuffed with ham, chicken and cream, sprinkled with cheese and baked or grilled

Trim the bases and cut off one third of the tops of

twelve young artichokes.

Boil in salted water for ten minutes; drain and remove the outside leaves until only the light green ones are left. Make a well in the centre of each one and liberally fill with the following mixture:

4 oz. ham and the pickings of a chicken (or about the same quantity as of minced ham).

Stir in

2 tablespoons cream
chopped parsley
salt, pepper and nutmeg.

Put the artichokes into a well-buttered oven-proof dish, sprinkle with grated Parmesan and bake in a very hot oven or under the grill for 10–15 minutes. Serve at once.

7 Carciofi alla Barigoule

Large artichokes braised with pork, mushrooms and white wine

Trim the bases and cut off half the tops of

6 large artichokes.

Boil for ten minutes, refresh in cold water and drain again. Remove the choke and fill with the following stuffing:

2 oz. minced pork
1 oz. minced bacon
1 small onion, chopped.

Stew these in a pan without colour; add

a little olive oil
8 oz. chopped mushrooms
salt and pepper.

Cook for five minutes, stirring from time to time.

Tie a rasher of bacon round each artichoke with string, put in an oven-proof dish with oil, fry lightly. Add a glass of white wine, the same of stock, cover and braise for just under an hour in a moderate oven. Remove the string and serve with the juices.

Asparagus/*Asparagi*

Of the many varieties grown in Italy, the commonest is the purple Genoa asparagus, in season from February through March into April.

It is a vegetable that should be simply served, but not one that is simple to cook. Having a woody stem and tender tip, it is easy to under- or overcook it. Nor are the tinned asparagus recommended as an easy way out; being necessarily soaked in liquid for some time, they have little texture or flavour. (The best I have found to be the large white Argenteuils.)

Freshness is always important, not least with asparagus, whose stems become woodier the longer they have been picked. The white stalks can be used for a soup.

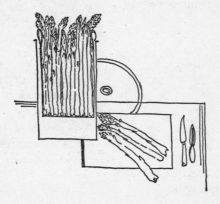

1   Asparagi

Asparagus; cold with vinaigrette; hot with Sauce Beurre Fondu or Sauce Mousseline

To be generous, allow one pound of asparagus for each person. Peel the lower white part with a potato peeler. Trim the bases and tie into loose bundles. Stand them upright in a deep pan and pour over boiling water, leaving the tips uncovered.
Salt well and cover. Boil for twenty minutes and drain; lay on a dish and serve hot or refresh carefully in cold water and drain again, if they are to be served cold.

Sauce Vinaigrette
(enough for six people)
In a bowl, put

a pinch of salt and pepper
a pinch of sugar
grated nutmeg
the juice of 1½ lemons
6 tablespoons good olive oil.

Mix thoroughly together and serve with the cold asparagus.

Beurre Fondu
In a small frying pan, put

6 oz. salted butter
a pinch of ground pepper
1 tablespoon cream.

Heat, shaking the pan until the butter and cream emulsifies. Serve at once with the asparagus.

Sauce Mousseline

Melt, but do not over-heat	*6 oz. butter.*
Beat over hot water	*4 egg yolks*
	juice of ½ a lemon
	1 egg white
	salt and pepper.

Beat well until fluffy and thickening. Remove the pan from the water and stir in the butter slowly and thoroughly. Return to the pan, still beating, until it is almost setting. Remove from the fire and fold in *a heaped tablespoon of whipped cream.*

Serve in a bowl with the hot asparagus.

2 Asparagi alla Wilhelmina

Asparagus with a slightly piquant butter sauce

Peel the white part of five or six pounds of asparagus. Tie loosely into bundles and trim the bases. Put into a deep pan and pour boiling water in up to the tips. Salt well and boil for twenty minutes. Drain and arrange in a long dish.

Meanwhile prepare the following sauce:

Melt in a frying pan — *4 oz. butter.*

Mix in — *1 level tablespoon flour.*

Cook for a minute, then stir in —
½ pint chicken broth
2 bayleaves
chopped parsley
juice of ¼ an onion
salt and pepper.

Bring to the boil and simmer for five minutes. Take the pan from the stove and whisk in —
3 egg yolks
juice of ½ a lemon.

Serve over the asparagus.

3 Asparagi alla Parmigiana

Asparagus with a butter and grated Parmesan sauce, finished under the grill

Cut off the green tips from four pounds of asparagus. Put into boiling salted water and cook for ten to fifteen minutes. Place in a dish and pour over them the following sauce:

Put into a frying pan

4 oz. butter
2 oz. grated Parmesan
2 tablespoons strong stock
ground pepper and nutmeg.

Stir until the sauce bubbles. Remove from the stove and add

2 beaten egg yolks.

Sprinkle with more grated Parmesan and colour quickly under the grill.

4 Asparagi alla crema

Asparagus with butter, cream and roast split almonds

Cut the white stalks off five pounds of asparagus and boil the green tips in boiling salted water for ten to fifteen minutes. (Reserve the white stalks for soup.)

Drain carefully, put into a shallow dish and pour over them the following sauce:

Into a frying-pan put

4 oz. butter
2 tablespoons cream.

Stir until mixture bubbles, add

juice of ¼ a lemon
ground pepper
3 oz. roast split almonds.

5   Asparagi all'Italiana

*Asparagus tips with coddled
eggs and cream*

Cut off the green tips of three pounds
of asparagus (reserve the white stalks
for soup). Boil in salted water for
ten to fifteen minutes and drain
carefully. Arrange the asparagus tips
in ramekins.

Break over them   *2 eggs.*

Season with   *salt and pepper*
and   *chopped chives (if available).*

Pour over   *a tablespoon cream.*

Pour a little hot water into the
bottom of a roasting tray, put in the
egg-dishes, cover with another tray
and bake in a hot oven for about
five minutes until the eggs are set.
They can also be cooked in a pan
with water over a gentle flame on
top of the stove.

6 Asparagi ai gamberi

Asparagus with prawns and lemon mayonnaise

Cut the green tips off four pounds of asparagus. Boil in salted water for ten to fifteen minutes and drain carefully. Arrange flat on a dish.

Pour over

a squeeze of lemon
2 tablespoons of oil
salt, pepper and nutmeg.

Allow to cool.

Peel and prepare the following sauce mayonnaise:

2 lb. large prawns.

Put in a bowl

3 egg yolks
salt and pepper
grated rind of ½ a lemon.

Stir and mix in slowly

½ pint olive oil.

Then add

the juice of the whole lemon.

Put the sauce in a pot, in the middle of a large dish, arrange the prawns round the pot and the asparagus round the prawns.

Beetroot/*Barbabietole*

How to boil beetroot
The smaller the beetroot, the sweeter and juicier they are. Wash them, taking care not to break the skin, which will let the juice out in the cooking.

Put them in a pan in cold water and bring to the boil. For small ones, boil for an hour; larger ones for two hours.

Place them in cold water for five minutes and then rub off the skin. Use as required.

1   Barbabietole alla panna   *Beetroot in cream*

Boil twelve small white or red beetroot. Cut into dice and pour over the following sauce:

Melt in a saucepan $\frac{1}{2}$ *oz. butter.*

Add $\frac{1}{2}$ *oz. flour.*

Cook for a few minutes.

Then stir in $\frac{1}{2}$ *pint single cream*
                                           salt and pepper
                                           chopped chives or spring onions.

Bring to the boil, stirring all the time, and cook gently for a few minutes.

2 Barbabietole alla Lionese

Beetroot baked with onions and milk

Slice ten small boiled beetroot into a basin.

Slice
and cook them in

2 onions
2 oz. butter.

Add

½ oz. flour
½ pint milk
salt, sugar and pepper.

Bring the sauce to the boil, stirring. Mix in the basin with the beetroot and lay in an oven-dish. Pour a little cream over and bake in a hot oven.

3 Beetroot Salad

Slice twelve small cooked beetroot on to a dish. Sprinkle with tarragon vinegar, salt and coarsely ground pepper.

Leave for a few hours and, when serving, add olive oil or cream.

4 Barbabietole alla Parmigiana

Small beetroots, baked whole with cream and Parmesan cheese

Peel eighteen very small cooked beetroot and put them into a buttered oven-dish.

Over them sprinkle

salt and pepper
½ pint single cream
chopped chives
2 oz. grated Parmesan
a few small knobs of butter.

Bake in a hot oven and serve, perhaps, with hot tongue.

Broad Beans/*Fave*

Beans and peas must be eaten young, for with age the sugar turns to starch and the skin toughens. Broad beans are best eaten when they are no bigger than a finger nail and the pod, which is usually no longer than four inches at this stage, can be cut and eaten as well. (See *alla Turca.*)

All the following recipes use the cooking liquid as part of the sauce; this preserves more of the flavour and nutriment. If the vegetable is found to be cooked before enough of the liquid has evaporated, drain the vegetable into another pan, boil the liquid fiercely and finish as the recipe requires.

---

1 Fave al burro *Broad beans cooked with ham*

Shell three pounds young broad beans. Put them in a saucepan with

a thick slice of ham
a stick of celery
parsley
3 cloves
twelve peppercorns
pinch of salt and a bayleaf.

Just cover with boiling water and boil fiercely for ten to fifteen minutes until the beans are cooked and the liquid has almost evaporated.

Remove the celery and other seasonings, chop up the ham and return it to the beans, and stir in

2 oz. butter.

---

2 Fave alla Turca

Take three pounds of young beans
no more than four inches long.

Cut each pod into three, putting
them into cold water as you cut them.

Boil in salted water for ten to fifteen
minutes, drain and mix in   *2 oz. butter, salt and pepper.*

3 Fave al vino

Shell three pounds of young broad
beans.

Put in a pan   *1 oz. butter*
and   *½ an onion finely chopped.*

When cooked stir in   *1 oz. flour.*

Then add the beans, and   *a sprig of chopped marjoram*
                                                    salt and pepper
                                                    1 teaspoon sugar
                                                    ¼ pint cheap white wine.

Just cover with stock and boil fiercely
until cooked.

4   Fave alla Romana

Shell three pounds of broad beans.

Stew in	*1 chopped onion* *2 tablespoons olive oil.*
Add	*a large sprig chopped sage* *1 dessertspoon tomato purée*

and the beans. Just cover with boiling water and boil fiercely until cooked and the juice has reduced. Serve hot or cold.

Broccoli Spears

The season for good broccoli spears in England (early spring) is short. They are picked when they are the size of a small cauliflower, fist size, with tightly bunched heads. They can be cooked whole when very small, or split into smaller heads with a small knife, prior to cooking.
They should be eaten simply, like asparagus.

1   Broccoli al burro

Take off most of the leaves and some of the stalk from four pounds of broccoli spears. Put them into plenty of boiling salted water and cook for about twenty minutes, taking care not to break the heads. Drain carefully and put into a serving dish.

Pour over
and sprinkle with

4 oz. butter
salt and rough ground
pepper.

2 Broccoli alla Parmigiana

Prepare and cook four pounds of broccoli in boiling salted water for about twenty minutes. Drain them carefully and lay them in an oven dish. Pour over the following sauce:

In a saucepan, put	½ oz. butter.
Heat and add	½ oz. flour.
Cook for a few minutes, then add	½ pint milk salt, pepper and nutmeg.
Bring to the boil, stirring well, then add	4 oz. grated Parmesan.

Cook for a few minutes. Pour the sauce over the broccoli. Sprinkle with more grated cheese and bake in a hot oven.

3   Broccoli all'Olandese

Prepare and cook four pounds of
broccoli spears for twenty minutes.
Drain them carefully and place on a
serving dish.

Meanwhile prepare the following
sauce:

Melt, but do not over-heat	*6 oz. butter.*
Beat over hot water together with	*4 egg yolks* *juice of half a lemon* *a small pinch cayenne.*

Beat the eggs until creamy and
thickening, remove from the hot
water and stir in the butter slowly
and thoroughly. Serve with
the broccoli.

Brussels Sprouts/*Cavolini di Brusselle*

1   Cavolini di Brusselle al limone

Wash two pounds of very small
brussels sprouts and cut off the outside
leaves. Boil in plenty of boiling
salted water for ten minutes until
cooked through. Drain and toss in a
pan with

the juice of a lemon
2 oz. butter
salt and a good sprinkling of
coarse ground pepper.

2 Cavolini di Brusselle alla Milanese

Prepare two pounds of very small brussels sprouts and cook them in plenty of boiling salted water for about ten minutes. Drain them well.

Heat
and
in a frying pan.

1 oz. butter
2 tablespoons olive oil

Add the sprouts and fry over a rather fierce heat, tossing frequently. When they are beginning to brown, add

1 oz. breadcrumbs
1 oz. grated Parmesan.

Continue to cook, taking care that the sprouts do not break up. Serve at once.

Cabbage/*Cavolo*

Cabbage is, perhaps, the most abused of all vegetables. If it is overcooked, it is quite useless for taste and food value. My publisher, Jock Murray, maintains that drinking cabbage water is excellent for general health and particularly for rheumatism. Cabbage, at any rate, deserves proper attention. Its cooking time will vary according to the type of cabbage, how fresh it is and how much stalk the leaves have. The general rule is to cook cabbage in plenty of boiling water, so that the water reboils quickly once the cabbage is added; alternatively it can be cooked (more usually the white or red cabbage) without any water at all.

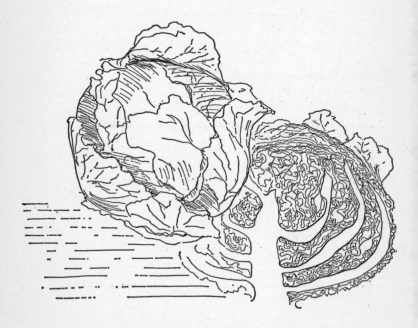

1 Cavolo al burro

Cut two large cabbages into six
segments each, and cut off most of
the stalk. Wash in cold water. Throw
into boiling water with salt for ten to
fifteen minutes, according to the type
of cabbage and how stalky the leaves
are. Drain at once, and mix in a pan
with melted butter, salt and pepper.

2 Cavolo alla panna

Cut one large white cabbage into four
and remove the stalks. Shred the
leaves across, not too finely. Wash in
cold water. Put into a pan of boiling
salted water for ten minutes, drain
well. Return it to the pan and add

*½ pint thin cream
salt, ground pepper and
nutmeg
1 dessertspoon grated
horseradish.*

Cover the pan with a lid and finish
cooking gently, stirring the cabbage
from time to time. If the cabbage has
made more juice, remove the lid
when nearly cooked, and boil fiercely
to reduce.

3   Cavolo al forno

Cut one large white cabbage (or
Savoy) into six segments and cut off
most of the stalk. Wash in cold water.
Blanch in boiling salted water
for ten minutes, drain and refresh
under cold water. Drain well.

Butter a shallow oven-dish, arrange
the segments of cabbage in it and add

salt and ground pepper
½ pint stock
4 oz. butter in nuts.

The stock should cover about a third
of the cabbage. Cover with
greaseproof paper and braise in a
fairly hot oven for about half an
hour, until cooked. Salt pork, ham,
sausages or garlic sausage, added
before the cabbage goes in the oven,
make a meal in itself.

4   Cavolo fritto

Cut one large white cabbage into
four and remove the stalk. Shred the
leaves across, not too finely. Blanch in
boiling salted water for five minutes,
drain well. Return to the pan with

4 oz. butter
salt and cayenne
4 crushed juniper berries
2 tablespoons vinegar.

Toss over a gentle fire until cooked.

5 Cavolo stufato

Prepare and blanch a white cabbage
as in the last recipe. Drain it.
Meanwhile cook
in

1 chopped onion
4 tablespoons olive oil.

Add

8 chopped tomatoes (or a tin)
salt and pepper
pinch of mixed herbs.

Add the cabbage to the sauce, cover
with a lid and finish cooking.

6 Cavolo alla Fiamminga

Cut two small red cabbages into four
and remove the stalk. Shred not too
finely and blanch in boiling salted
water for five minutes. Drain well
and return to the pan with

4 oz. butter
a grated onion
2 oz. chopped lean bacon
2 cloves
bayleaf, salt and pepper.

Cook gently for about twenty
minutes until cooked. Remove the
bayleaf and cloves.

7 Cavolo alla Tedesca

Cut two small red cabbages into four
and remove the stalk. Shred, not too
finely, and blanch in boiling salted
water for five minutes. Drain well
and return to the pan with

4 oz. butter
salt and pepper
sprinkling of caraway seeds
2 tablespoons wine vinegar
1 grated onion.

Finish cooking over a gentle heat for
about twenty minutes.

8 Cavolo ripieno

Cabbage leaves stuffed with spinach and mushrooms

Cut off the main stalk of a large green
cabbage (preferably Savoy), and
remove the leaves. Blanch the leaves
in boiling salted water for five
minutes and drain well. Cut any thick
stalk from the leaves and fill with
the following:

¼ lb. chopped cooked spinach
¼ lb. chopped cooked
mushrooms
3 egg yolks
4 oz. fresh breadcrumbs
salt and pepper
2 oz. grated cheese.

Wrap this mixture in the leaves and
braise in stock and butter in a
moderate oven for about half an hour.

Capsicums (Peppers)/*Peperoni*

Peeling peppers is by no means easy, particularly in England, where the peppers are not freshly picked. They can be plunged into boiling fat for a minute but the result is not always satisfactory. The skins, however, may be left on, providing the peppers are as firm and as fresh as possible. It is left to the discretion of the cook whether they be peeled or not.

1   Peperoni alla Spagnuola

Cut six peppers (red, green and
yellow, if possible) in half and
remove the seeds. Cut into thick
strips

Heat, in a deep frying pan	*¼ pint olive oil.*
In it, fry	*2 sliced onions*
	2 large cloves garlic (chopped)
and	*the sliced peppers.*
When almost cooked, add	*8 chopped tomatoes (or a tin)*
	salt and pepper.

Finish cooking for another ten
minutes, until the peppers are still
slightly crisp. This can be eaten hot
or cold.

2 Peperoni farciti

Peppers filled with chicken, rice and thyme and braised

Cut off the stalk end of six large peppers and remove the seeds. Cook in boiling salted water for ten minutes; drain and fill with the following risotto:

Fry, in olive oil

1 chopped onion.

Add

½ lb. chopped cooked chicken 4 oz. rice.

Fry for a few minutes, then add

½ pint chicken stock chopped thyme salt and pepper.

Cook for about 12 minutes until the rice begins to swell, then fill the peppers three-quarters full with rice and stock.

Put the peppers, open end up, carefully in a dish, sprinkle with olive oil and stock, and bake in a hot oven for twenty to thirty minutes. Serve hot or cold.

3   Peperoni farciti

Peppers with pork, herbs and cheese

Cut six peppers in half and remove the seeds. Fill the halves with the following stuffing:

1 lb. pork sausage meat
2 eggs
salt, pepper and nutmeg
chopped chives
chopped marjoram.

On each pepper place

a thick slice of Emmenthal cheese.

Put them in an oven dish with pieces of butter and a little stock and bake in a moderate oven for about half an hour.

4   Peperoni fritti

Deep-fried slices of peppers with tomato and basil sauce

Cut six peppers in half and remove the seeds. Cut the peppers into half again lengthwise and dip them into this batter:

Make a well in

2 tablespoons flour.

Add

1 egg yolk
1 tablespoon olive oil.

Mix and start stirring in the flour, adding

3 tablespoons water
a pinch of salt and pepper

until the batter is like thick cream.

Deep fry the slices of pepper in this batter and serve with the following sauce:

Fry, in olive oil

1 chopped onion (small)
1 clove garlic (small).

When cooked, add

8 chopped tomatoes (or a tin)
salt and pepper
1 teaspoon chopped basil.

Cardoons/*Cardi*

Cardoons are the top stalks of thistle artichokes, delicious in flavour. They should be grown with the earth piled high so that the stalks remain white.

1 Cardi al burro

Peel three pounds of cardoons and cut them in two lengthwise, putting them into cold water as they are prepared, to keep them white. Cook in boiling salted water for ten to fifteen minutes, drain and toss in butter and a little more salt and pepper.

2 Cardi in umido

Peel three pounds of cardoons and cut them into two-inch lengths. Blanch in salted water for five minutes. Drain, and dip in flour. Fry in olive oil until brown and cooked. Put into a serving dish, sprinkle with lemon juice and cheese.

Carrots / *Carote*

1   Carote all'aceto   *Carrots with vinegar*

Peel six large carrots, cut them into
four lengthways, and remove some of
the hard centre core. Cut into inch
pieces, put into a shallow saucepan
and just cover with

cold water
2 bayleaves
3 tablespoons wine vinegar
½ minced onion
3 crushed juniper berries
a little salt and pepper.

Bring to the boil and boil fiercely
until the liquid has almost gone and
the carrots are cooked. Sprinkle with
chopped parsley and serve hot or
cold.

2   Carote al vermouth   *Glazed carrots in vermouth*

Wash and peel six large carrots.
Quarter them lengthways, cut out the
hard centre and dice the remainder.

Put the carrots into a thick pan with   *2 oz. butter*
and a pinch of   *salt and pepper and sugar.*

Set the carrots in the butter for three
minutes.

Then add   *1 wineglass cheap white*
                                               vermouth.

Cover the pan and stew the carrots
rather gently, shaking the pan from
time to time. Add a little water if
the carrots get dry. When the
carrots are tender (about twenty-five
minutes) remove the lid and bubble
up the liquid until it thickens to a
syrup. Empty into a dish and sprinkle
with parsley. The syrupy effect of
this dish is not always so easy to
achieve, due, I think, to how much
moisture there is in the carrots. For
the final stage, when the carrots are
tender (if dry) sprinkle lightly with
sugar and add a little more vermouth
and toss over a good flame to
caramelize. This is a good dish with
pork and lamb.

3   Carote alla Parmigiana

Carrots and celery with Parmesan

Wash and peel six large carrots and three outside sticks of celery. Quarter the carrots lengthwise, cut out the hard centre and dice the remainder. Dice the celery and put both into a pan. Just cover with cold water, add chicken bouillon to season and bring to the boil. Simmer until tender. Strain the carrots and celery, keeping the cooking liquor. Put the carrots and celery into a dish and make a velouté sauce with the stock:

In a saucepan melt	*1 oz. butter.*
Add and mix in	*1 oz. flour.*

Cook the roux and add the stock, bring to the boil and reduce until the sauce is the thickness of double cream.

Then stir in	*1 oz. grated Parmesan*
and	*1 oz. grated cheddar.*

Pour the sauce over the carrots and celery, sprinkle with Parmesan cheese and bake in a hot oven for ten minutes. (This can be prepared in advance and baked when required for fifteen to twenty minutes.)

4   Carote alla casalinga

Top, tail and wash three pounds of
very young carrots. Put them into a
pan with cold water and salt. Bring to
the boil and half cook for five
minutes. Drain them and return to
the pan with

4 oz. butter
salt, pepper and sugar
pinch of rosemary.

Cover with a lid and stew over a
gentle flame until cooked. Then add,
away from the stove,

3 tablespoons stock
juice of $\frac{1}{2}$ a lemon
3 egg yolks, beaten.

Shake the pan until the sauce
thickens, put into a dish and
sprinkle with chopped parsley.

5   Carote al forno

Trim two pounds of medium-sized
carrots, scrape them and put in a pan
of cold water to boil. Parboil for ten
minutes, drain and lay in a buttered
oven dish. Half-cover with stock,
sprinkle with salt, pepper, pinch of
thyme and small pieces of butter.

Braise in a rather hot oven, basting
from time to time, until cooked.

Cauliflower/*Cavolfiori*

1 Cavolfiori al burro

The best cauliflowers have small,
tightly-packed white heads. Trim the
outside leaves of three very small or
two larger cauliflowers. Cut a cross
into the thick base of the stem. Wash
in cold water. Put into a pan with
plenty of cold water and add salt and
pepper. Bring to the boil and cook
carefully for twenty or so minutes
(longer for a very large cauliflower).
Drain with care and put on a dish in a
warm oven. Prepare a butter sauce
with:

2 oz. butter
1 tablespoon wine vinegar or
lemon
salt and coarsely ground pepper
chopped parsley.

Put the ingredients in a small pan, let
them bubble up, without separating,
and pour over the cauliflower.

2 Cavolfiori alla Parmigiana

Trim two medium or three very
small cauliflowers and cut a cross in
the stem. Cover with plenty of salted
cold water and boil for about twenty
minutes. Drain with care, put on to a
dish and pour over the following
cheese sauce:

Heat   *1 oz. butter.*

Add   *1 oz. flour*
and cook.

Add   *1 pint milk.*

Stir, bring to the boil and cook for
a few minutes.

Add and blend   *salt and pepper*
                                                  grated nutmeg
                                                  2 oz. grated cheese
                                                  1 dessertspoon French
                                                  mustard.

Pour the sauce over the cauliflower,
sprinkle with more grated cheese and
brown in a very hot oven.

3 Cavolfiori fritti

Cut off the leaves of two medium
cauliflowers and cut off the 'flowers'
where they join the main core. Put
into a pan of cold water and parboil
for ten minutes. Dip each piece in
beaten egg and breadcrumbs and fry
in half butter, half oil. Sprinkle with
grated cheese before serving.

4 Cavolfiori alla Piemontese

*'Flowers' of cauliflowers
cooked with onion, anchovy
and marjoram*

Remove the flowers from two
medium-sized cauliflowers and parboil
them for ten minutes. Drain them and
return to the pan with

*1 small grated onion
6 finely chopped anchovies
1 tablespoon vinegar
¼ pint olive oil
chopped marjoram.*

Cover with a lid. Cook for a few
minutes and serve hot or cold.

Celery/*Sedano*

Choose fat heads of celery, not too long and stringy, nor brown from frost or being packed too tight. The very outside leaves and stalks can be used for soups and stocks.

1   Sedano fritto

Remove the outer stalks and cut off the leaves of three heads of celery. Cut into two-inch lengths and wash the pieces well in cold water. Parboil in salted water for fifteen minutes but it should still be crisp. Drain, dip in egg and breadcrumbs and fry in half butter, half oil.

2   Sedano all'Italiana

Celery, thyme and tomatoes

Remove the outer stalks of two large heads of celery and cut off the leaves. Cut into inch lengths and wash well.

Into a deep frying-pan put

¼ pint olive oil
1 chopped onion
the pieces of celery.

Fry until the celery is golden and almost cooked, then add

¼ pint tomato juice
salt and pepper
little chopped thyme.

Cook for another few minutes and serve.

3   Sedano al forno

Celery braised with ham and bayleaves

Remove the outside stalks and cut off the green leaves of three celery heads. Trim the roots and cut them into four, lengthways, Parboil in salted water for ten minutes, drain and lay on a buttered oven-dish with

6 oz. chopped ham or bacon
coarsely ground pepper
1 pint stock (half-way up celery)
3 bayleaves
small pieces of butter.

Cook in a rather hot oven for twenty to thirty minutes.

4   Sedano alla Greca

Remove the outer stalks and cut off
the leaves of three heads of celery.
Cut into two-inch lengths and wash
well in cold water. Parboil for ten
minutes in salted water, drain and
put into a deep frying pan with

½ pint stock
juice of a lemon
4 tablespoons olive oil
3 bayleaves
1 tablespoon coriander seeds
a little salt and pepper.

Cook over a moderate fire until tender
and the stock has reduced. Serve hot
or cold.

Celeriac

1 Celeriac 'remoulade'

Peel a medium-sized celeriac root
with a knife, cutting away any brown
patches. Slice it on a mandolin (or
finely with a sharp knife) and shred
into long matchsticks. Mix, at once,
with the following sauce:

In a bowl, put

2 egg yolks
1 tablespoon tarragon vinegar
2 tablespoons French mustard
salt and pepper.

Gradually add

2 tablespoons olive oil
2 tablespoons thick cream.

Chicory/*Cicoria*

1 Cicoria brasata *Braised chicory*

Wash one and a half pounds of chicory and if they are thick, split them down the middle into two, three or four. Lay them in a flat baking dish with

2 oz. butter in nuts
1 cup stock or water and chicken bouillon
salt and pepper to taste
juice of a ½ lemon
1 teaspoon sugar.

Bring the liquid to the boil, cover the pan and cook in a fairly hot oven for ten minutes with the lid, and a further ten to fifteen minutes with the lid off. Sprinkle with chopped parsley and serve.

2   Cicoria con prosciutto

Chicory and ham

6 very thin slices of ham
12 pieces of cooked chicory

Cut the slices of ham in two and wrap
each half round the chicory, laying
them in a buttered dish. Pour over a
Sauce Mornay, sprinkle with cheese
and bake in a hot oven for twenty
minutes.

Sauce Mornay

Melt

1 oz. butter.

Add and cook

1 oz. flour.

Add gradually

*¾ pint milk or milk and single
cream.*

Add

*2 oz. grated cheddar
salt, pepper and nutmeg.*

Bring to the boil, and pour over the
chicory.

3 Tortino di cicoria   *Chicory tart*

Line a six-inch flan dish with short
pastry. Roughly chop three pieces of
cooked chicory.

Lay them in the flan.

In a bowl mix

> *2 eggs*
> *2 oz. grated cheddar*
> *¼ pint milk*
> *¼ pint single cream*
> *pinch of salt, pepper and
> nutmeg.*

Pour the mixture over the chicory in
the flan and bake in a moderate oven
for about thirty minutes until the
cheese and egg has set. Makes a good
simple meal with cold ham and a
green salad.

4 Insalata di cicoria

Chicory salad with hazelnut dressing

Roughly chop three pieces of chicory and put into a salad bowl.

Toss with a dressing made as follows:

In a cup put

*1 tablespoon crushed hazelnuts
pinch of salt and pepper
pinch of sugar
1 juice of a lemon
4 oz. fluid cream.*

Mix the dressing thoroughly and dress the chicory. Do not leave the chicory too long undressed – it will discolour. Sprinkle with chopped parsley and surround the bowl with washed watercress.

Courgettes/*Zucchini*

Courgettes are baby marrows, easily grown, and, I would think, becoming more popular than the large marrows. The season is the summer, the end of June through to September.

Courgettes survive several days after being picked because of their high water content; and for the same reason are preferably cooked without water.

The flowers (male and female), though without marked flavour, make excellent eating. They should be prepared within a few hours of picking to prevent them wilting.

1   Zucchini al burro

Courgettes cooked with a little water and butter in a covered pan

Wash two and a half pounds of *small* courgettes and trim off the stems.

Put them in a thick saucepan with

2 fluid oz. water
4 oz. butter
salt and ground pepper.

Cover with a lid and place on a low fire, tossing the pan until the courgettes are very nearly soft (*al dente*).

Serve in a hot dish with plenty of

chopped parsley
and a squeeze of lemon.

2   Zucchini al pomodoro

Courgettes cooked with onion, garlic and tomatoes

Wash two and a half pounds of
courgettes and trim off the stems.
Cut them into inch lengths and put
them in a deep frying pan with

1 medium sliced onion
2 cloves garlic chopped
4 tablespoons olive oil
a little salt and pepper.

Cover with a lid and stew for ten
minutes, stirring from time to time.
Remove the lid, turn up the heat and
fry until slightly golden.

Add

a half-kilo tin of Italian
tomatoes or
1 lb. peeled ripe tomatoes.

Add more

salt and pepper.

Cook for a few moments longer only.
Serve hot with roast meat or cold
with fish salad.

3 Zucchini farciti

Courgettes stuffed with spinach and cream cheese and grilled

There are two methods for preparing the courgettes for this dish, depending on their size.

If they are small, and therefore difficult to stuff, it is better to cook them in butter and a little water and then slit them ready for the stuffing. Allow four for each person as a beginning or six as a main-course lunch dish.

If they are larger (about six inches) trim off the stems and 'core' them carefully with an apple corer.

In either case fill them with the following stuffing:

Soften in a bowl near the stove — *3 demi-sel cheeses.*

Cook, for a few minutes — *1 lb. prepared spinach or a packet of frozen leaf spinach.*

Refresh under cold water, squeeze dry and chop.

Add — *1 whole egg*
salt, pepper and nutmeg.

Mix all the above ingredients together
and stuff the courgettes. (If the
courgettes are cored, force the
mixture in with a piping bag or small
spoon.)

The cooked courgettes have their
cooking liquor poured over them;
sprinkle them with grated Parmesan
cheese and brown under the grill.

The large courgettes, cored, stuffed
and ready for cooking, are laid in a
dish with a little water, butter and
seasoning and baked in a moderate
oven. When cooked, sprinkle with
grated Parmesan and finish under the
grill.

4 Fiori di Zucchini ripieni al pilaf

A beginning dish of courgette flowers filled with a saffron and cayenne pilaf and deep-fried, served with tomato sauce

Allow two to three flowers per person.

Fill them with the following pilaf:

Heat in a thick pan	*2 tablespoons olive oil.*
Add	*a small pinch of crushed saffron.* *4 oz. patna rice* *a pinch of cayenne pepper* *1 teaspoon paprika.*
Fry the ingredients without browning the rice, then add	*⅟ pint boiling stock* *salt.*

Simmer until the rice is very nearly cooked and allow to cool.

Meanwhile, prepare the following batter:

Put in a bowl	*2 heaped tablespoons flour.*
Make a well, add	*1 egg* *1 tablespoon olive oil* *pepper and salt.*
Mix together and start stirring in until the batter is a thickish cream.	*3 tablespoons water*

Dip the stuffed flowers into the
batter, drain and deep fry until golden.

Serve the following sauce separately:

Put in a saucepan

*twelve sliced tomatoes (or a tin
Italian tomatoes).
1 tablespoon olive oil
½ grated onion
salt and a little sugar.*

Cook until creamy and pass through a
sieve.

5   **Fiori di Zucchini ripieni di pollo**   *Courgette flowers stuffed with chicken*

Allow two or three flowers per person and fill them with a tablespoonful of the following mixture:

Make a roux with

1½ oz. flour
1½ oz. butter.

Cook until sandy; add gradually

½ pint milk
pepper and nutmeg
a nut of chicken bouillon.

Simmer for five minutes (the sauce should be thick) and then mix in

4 oz. finely chopped ham
8 oz. finely chopped cooked chicken.

Cover with greaseproof paper and allow the mixture to get cold.

Dip the stuffed flowers in a batter made in the same way as in the previous recipe.

Deep-fry them, turning them once or twice and serve on a napkin with segments of lemon and watercress.

Cucumber/*Cetriolo*

1 Cetriolo alla Comasca

Cut some strips of peel from a
cucumber and slice the cucumber
very fine on a mandolin. Arrange on
a dish and sprinkle over

½ an onion grated (or very
finely chopped)
1 tablespoon tarragon vinegar
2 tablespoons good olive oil.

Allow it to 'pickle' for fifteen minutes
before serving.

2 Cetriolo condito al miele

Cucumber with honey
dressing

Cut some strips from a cucumber, cut
the cucumber into inch pieces and
then into rather thin wedges. Pour
over the following dressing:

1 full teaspoon honey
salt and pepper
pinch chopped marjoram
2 tablespoons wine vinegar
4 tablespoons olive oil.

3   Cetriolo al burro

Cucumber cooked with butter, chervil and lemon

Cut strips of peel from two cucumbers, cut the cucumbers into two-inch pieces and then into thick wedges.

Put them in a thick pan with

4 oz. butter
1 cup water
large pinch chervil.

Cover with a lid and stew gently for fifteen minutes.

Meanwhile, with a very sharp knife, cut the skin and pith from

2 lemons.

Then cut out the segments from the dividing skin. Add the segments of the lemons to the cucumber, squeeze the skins over and shake the pan over a gentle heat.

Add

2 oz. of butter in pieces.

Remove from the stove and shake again.

Serve with a meat dish that is cooked with fruit, such as lamb basted with honey or pork with apricots.

4   Cetriolo alla Spagnuola

*Stuffed cucumbers, tied and
baked with onions, carrots
and thyme*

Cut strips of peel from two
cucumbers. Cut the cucumbers into
two lengthways.

With a teaspoon, remove some of the
seeds, the length of the cucumber.
Fill with the following mixture and
tie the two halves together:

*8 oz. minced ham
8 oz. cooked minced chicken
or meat
salt, pepper and nutmeg
pinch chopped thyme
1 egg.*

In a long casserole fry in oil

*2 sliced onions
3 chopped carrots.*

When almost cooked, remove and
fry the cucumbers. Return the onions
and carrots and add

*6 halved tomatoes
a small sprig thyme
6 peppercorns
a little salt.*

Cover the casserole and bake in a
moderate oven for half an hour, until
the cucumbers are cooked. Remove
the cucumbers. Pass the remainder
through a sieve or Mouli. Remove the
string from the cucumbers and pour
the sauce over them.

5   Cetriolo alla Toscana

*Cucumber cooked with
butter, cream and nutmeg*

Cut strips of peel from two
cucumbers and cut into thick slices.

Put them in a pan with

*4 oz. butter
1 cup water
salt and pepper.*

Cook over a rather gentle heat
without a lid, and when nearly
cooked add

*1 cup cream
½ nutmeg grated.*

Shake the pan over the fire until the
cream thickens, empty into a dish
and sprinkle with paprika.

Egg-plant (Aubergines)/*Melanzane*

Vegetables that are foreign to England were viewed with the utmost suspicion by the medieval herbalists. Egg-plants were called 'mad' or 'raging' apples and I imagine were scarce indeed. But they have always made a colourful impact in continental market displays and are obtainable in England, more or less, all the year round. Their colour is unique among vegetables and the capacity of the flesh to absorb oil and juices makes the egg-plant valuable in a vegetable stew or cooked with spices.

1 Melanzane fritte

Choose three large, firm egg-plants
of a smooth dark colour. Cut off the
peel and stalk and cut into thick slices.
Put them in a colander with a
sprinkling of salt and leave for half an
hour so that some of the bitter juice
may escape.

Meanwhile, prepare the following
batter:

In a bowl put	*2 heaped tablespoons flour.*
Make a well; add	*1 egg* *salt and pepper* *1 tablespoon olive oil.*
Start stirring in the flour and gradually add until you have a thick, creamy consistency.	*3 tablespoons water*

Dip the pieces of egg-plant in this
and deep-fry for about five minutes.

Serve with a tomato sauce, made simply with	*twelve sliced tomatoes* *2 crushed cloves of garlic* *salt and pepper* *bayleaf* *1 tablespoon olive oil.*

Cook these until creamy and pass
through a sieve.

2   Melanzane alla griglia, Genovese

Grilled egg-plant with a basil and garlic sauce

Peel three large egg-plants and cut off the stalks. Cut into thick slices, diagonally, almost the length of the egg-plant. Put into a colander with a sprinkling of salt to draw out the bitter juices.

Then season with

2 tablespoons flour
salt and coarsely ground
pepper.

Light the grill in advance, brush the grill tray with oil. Then dip the pieces of egg-plant in the flour and lay them on the grill; brush with oil. Grill on both sides, brushing with olive oil as they cook. Keep in a hot oven until they have all been grilled. Serve with the following *pesto* sauce. (*Pesto* can be bought in tins – use it sparingly.)

Pound in a mortar to a fine paste

3 cloves of garlic
2 sprigs of basil
4 chopped walnuts.

Gradually work in

2 tablespoons olive oil.

3 Melanzane al forno

Egg-plant cooked with tomato, garlic, breadcrumbs and Parmesan cheese

Peel three large egg-plants and cut off their stalks. Slice obliquely and put into a colander with a sprinkling of salt until the bitter juice is drawn out.

Meanwhile, peel and slice   *twelve tomatoes.*

Crush over them   *3 cloves garlic*
and make a mixture of   *2 oz. breadcrumbs*
                                             1 grated lemon rind
                                             2 oz. grated Parmesan.

Pour a little olive oil into the bottom of a large, fairly shallow oven-dish, arrange layers of egg-plant and tomato, add a little more olive oil, press down and sprinkle with the breadcrumbs and Parmesan.

Bake in a rather hot oven for about half an hour. Serve very hot (with, perhaps, a grilled steak).

4   Insalata di Melanzane

A salad of sliced egg-plant and tomatoes, cooked in white wine

Peel three large egg-plants and cut off the stalks. Slice fairly thick and leave in a colander with a sprinkling of salt to draw out the juices.

Meanwhile peel and slice   *twelve tomatoes.*

Heat some olive oil in a frying pan (until very hot) and fry the egg-plants in it, turning rather quickly, for they will easily take colour. Keep those that are cooked to one side, if there are too many for one pan.

Put them in the pan and pour over   *1 glass white wine.*

Add   *2 cloves crushed garlic*
and a little   *chopped basil.*

Let it bubble and reduce and then empty the pan over the sliced tomatoes and arrange on a dish when cold.

Fennel/*Finocchio*

Bulb fennel is nowadays quite regularly imported to England, which is fortunate as it is a difficult plant to grow. The failure seems to be lack of fine weather at the moment when the plant is about to fill out, resulting in the fine feathery sprays of the herb fennel.

The bulb should be firm and white; discoloration and dryness of the outer sheaths indicate old age, which, alas, can happen with the time lapse in transport from abroad. The outer sheathes may then need peeling or removing. The green shoots and leaves are cut to the top of the bulb – these can be happily used as a flavouring for another dish. The flavour of fennel, cooked and uncooked, varies in the same way as celery, and there are many who prefer the raw flavour. Fennel fritters, however, fried crisp and brown, have a fine nutty taste and go very well with a grilled fish.

In Italy bulb fennel has many uses in a salad; very often a few slivers are mixed with the winter radish leaves or appear chopped on top of a tomato salad. In this way it is used for its crispness and as a secondary flavour. On its own it is best cut very thin and served with a pot of best oil and vinegar and seasoning, separate. This, as an accompaniment to a fine goat's cheese, both fennel and cheese being sprinkled with oil and pepper, makes an excellent end to a meal.

1 Finocchi al burro *Fennel with butter*

Trim the top shoots of four medium-
sized bulbs of fennel and peel the
outer sheathes with a potato peeler
(if they are white and young, this is
not necessary). Trim the base and cut the
fennel first in half and then each half
into three or four. Wash the segments
well and cook them in boiling salted
water (with a small piece of lemon to
keep the colour) for about twenty
minutes, until just tender.

Meanwhile melt in a casserole   *1 oz. butter*
and grate into it   *½ onion.*

Strain the cooked fennel, drain well
and toss in the butter. Sprinkle with
grated Parmesan and serve in the
casserole. A good dish to go with
slices of veal with Marsala sauce.

2   Fritto di finocchi   *Fennel fritters with lemon*

Trim three or four bulbs of fennel
and cut them first in half and then in
thin segments, each piece held
together by the stalk.

Heat the oil in the deep-fryer and
make the following batter:

In a bowl put	*1 heaped tablespoon flour.*
Make a well; add	*1 egg white*
	1 tablespoon olive oil.
Stir in	*½ cup water (tepid)*
and season with	*salt and pepper.*

Dip the pieces of fennel individually
into the batter (the batter should coat
the fennel but not cling in quantity
to it nor contain too much water,
which will make the batter
disintegrate in the fat).

Fry the fennel until crisp and brown,
drain and place on a dish with a
paper napkin (keep in a warm oven
while the remainder are fried).
Serve with good-sized pieces of
lemon.

3 Finocchi al forno

Fried fennel with tomatoes and garlic with a crisp topping

Trim the tops and bases of four fennel bulbs. Halve the bulbs and cut into thin segments into a thick shallow gratin dish (or frying pan).

Heat

½ cup olive oil.

Into the oil put

1 onion thinly sliced
2 chopped cloves of garlic.

Fry for a minute or two and add the fennel. Continue frying, stirring occasionally with a wooden spoon. When the fennel is beginning to brown and is almost cooked add

one twelve-oz. tin of Italian peeled tomatoes, broken up
salt and ground pepper.

Lower the heat and infuse for five minutes.

This initial cooking can be done in advance.

Sprinkle the following topping over the fennel in the gratin dish (or transfer into a gratin dish from the frying pan)

½ cup breadcrumbs, roughly crushed
½ cup grated Parmesan
½ grated rind of lemon
1 chopped clove garlic.

Bake in a hot oven until crisp.

French Beans/*Fagiolini*

The best variety are the very small *mange-tout* beans, which are no more than two inches long. The stringless variety are more common and should not be more than three or four inches long and very green.

1 Fagiolini al burro or vinaigrette

Boil two pounds young French beans in plenty of salted water for ten to fifteen minutes (according to their size). Drain them, add 2 oz. butter, salt and pepper and toss.

For serving cold, drain the beans once cooked, refresh quickly in cold water and drain again. Then mix with the following *Sauce Vinaigrette*:

Mix together

1 tablespoon white wine vinegar
3 tablespoons good olive oil
salt, pepper and a pinch of sugar
2 chopped spring onions.

2 Fagiolini alla crema

Boil two pounds of young French beans in plenty of salted water for ten minutes until still slightly crisp. Drain and put into a saucepan with

a pinch of salt, pepper and sugar
a sprinkling of chopped chives and parsley
¼ pint cream
2 egg yolks.

Heat gently together, stirring, for five minutes, but do not boil.

3   Fagiolini allo Zabaglione

French beans with a fluffy egg and butter sauce

Boil two pounds of young French beans in plenty of salted water for ten minutes until still slightly crisp. Drain and put in a dish. Meanwhile prepare the following sauce:

Put in a pan over hot water

3 egg yolks
1 tablespoon white wine vinegar
1 teaspoon sugar
pinch of all-spice.

Beat until fluffy. Then add

2 tablespoons cream.

Pour over the beans. Very good with boiled ham.

4   Fagiolini in fricassea

French beans with a little garlic and basil

Boil two pounds of young French beans in plenty of salted water for about ten minutes. Drain and serve with the following:

In a frying pan, heat up

2 tablespoons olive oil
1 clove garlic, squeezed
1 teaspoon chopped basil
salt and pepper.

Add the beans and toss in the sauce. Serve very hot.

Haricot Beans/*Fagioli*

1 Fagioli alla Romana

Haricot beans with oil, anchovies and lemon

Use the new season's dried beans; some commercial beans can be old to the point that they never soften. Soak one pound of haricot beans overnight in plenty of cold water. In the morning, drain and re-fill with cold water. Bring slowly to the boil without salt. Boil for about one and a half hours or until tender, seasoning with salt half-way through.

Meanwhile finely slice

3 onions.

Brown them in
then add

3 tablespoons olive oil
6 chopped anchovies
salt, pepper and nutmeg
some of the cooking liquor
juice of a lemon
chopped parsley.

Mix with the beans and serve very hot.

2   Fagioli alla Fiorentina

Haricot beans with chopped fresh herbs and velouté sauce

Soak one pound of haricot beans in plenty of cold water, overnight. Drain, refill with cold water, and bring slowly to the boil without salt. Cook for about one and a half hours until tender, seasoning half-way through with salt. Meanwhile make the following velouté sauce:

Melt in a saucepan — *1½ oz. butter.*

Add — *1½ oz. flour.*

Cook for a few minutes.

Then add — *1½ pints chicken broth.*

Bring to the boil and cook for a few minutes. Remove the pan from the fire and add

*juice of a lemon
3 egg yolks
1 tablespoon mixed herbs.*

Mix the sauce with the drained beans and serve with boiled chicken.

3 Fagioli alla polenta

Purée of haricot beans with butter and cream

Soak one pound of haricot beans in
plenty of cold water, overnight.
Drain and re-fill with cold water.
Bring slowly to the boil without
salt and cook for about one and a half
hours until tender, adding salt half-
way through. Drain and pass them
through a sieve or Mouli. Then add

4 oz. butter
¼ pint cream
salt, pepper and nutmeg.

Cover with lid or paper and put in
the oven for ten minutes.

4 Crocchette di fagioli

Croquettes of haricot beans

Make a purée of haricot beans (as in
the last recipe) and put it in a
saucepan with

1 egg
4 oz. butter
*1 tablespoon white wine
vinegar*
chopped balm mint
salt and pepper.

Mix well and allow to cool. Roll up
into balls or little sausages, dip them
in egg and breadcrumbs and fry them
in a frying pan in a little butter and oil.

Jerusalem Artichokes/*Carciofi di Giudea*

Jerusalem artichokes are a tall leafy plant with very irregular bulbous roots. They are difficult to peel without wasting a good deal of the artichoke; it is thus easier to cook them first and peel them when they have cooled a little. Their flavour is slightly sweet and they become almost opaque when cooked.

1 Purée di carciofi di Giudea *Purée of Jerusalem artichokes*

In a saucepan put

2 oz. butter
1 sliced onion
2 lb. washed chopped artichokes
2 sticks celery
2 bayleaves
salt and pepper.

Cover with a lid and stew gently on the stove for twenty minutes. Pass through a Mouli. Mix with a little thin cream to make a purée or with about 1 pint milk to make a soup.

2 Carciofi di Giudea alla Parmigiana

Peel two pounds of Jerusalem artichokes and boil them in salt water for about twenty minutes. Drain and cut into fairly thick slices.

Meanwhile prepare a white sauce:

Make a roux with	$\frac{3}{4}$ oz. butter $\frac{3}{4}$ oz. flour.
Heat in a saucepan	$\frac{1}{2}$ pint milk $\frac{1}{2}$ peeled onion a pinch or small bunch of mixed herbs.
Mix the strained milk into the roux and when it thickens and boils, reduce the heat and add	4 oz. grated cheese (Parmesan, Emmenthal or Cheddar).

Stir the cheese in, add a little cream if the sauce is too thick, and mix into the sliced artichokes. Sprinkle with grated Parmesan cheese and bake in a hot oven for fifteen minutes.

Leeks/*Porri*

1 Porri alla casalinga

Cut off most of the green part and
the root of two and a half pounds of
leeks. Slit them, not all the way
through, from the root up and wash
thoroughly. Put into boiling salted
water for five minutes. Drain and
refresh in cold water.

Smear a shallow baking dish with
dripping; arrange the leeks in it; add

little pieces of dripping
a sprinkling of sugar
salt and crushed pepper
a pinch of mixed herbs.

Then barely cover with
and braise in a moderate oven for
thirty to forty minutes.

stock

2 Porri alla crema

Prepare six good-sized leeks and wash
them well (cut off most of the green,
the roots and slit them half-way
through). Blanch them in boiling
salted water for ten minutes and
drain them.

Cut each leek into four, lengthways,
and arrange them in the bottom of a
buttered, shallow oven-dish.

Sprinkle with *coarsely ground peppercorns*
salt

and pour over *½ pint cream (thin).*

Bake in a moderate oven for twenty
minutes to half an hour. Sprinkle
with parsley.

3 Porri alla Greca

Prepare six good-sized leeks and wash
them well (cut off most of the green,
the roots and slit them half-way
through). Cut them into four,
lengthways, and put in a large frying
pan or oven-dish with

$\frac{1}{4}$ *cup olive oil*
2 oz. coriander seeds
1 cup white wine
1 cup water
salt and pepper
3 bayleaves.

Bring to the boil on top of the stove
and cook without a lid, stirring
carefully until the leeks are cooked
and the juice is reduced. Serve hot or
cold.

Lentils|*Lenticchie*

Lentils need not be soaked before being cooked, but a few hours in cold water often helps, for the longer the lentils have been stored, the more dehydrated they can become.

1 Lenticchie alla corona

Lentils cooked with pork knuckles and anchovies

In a pan, put

1 lb. lentils
2 knuckles pork
2 onions, sliced
1 carrot, sliced
6 peppercorns
2 bayleaves
2 pints stock.

Bring to the boil, skim and simmer gently until the pork and lentils are cooked (about one and a half hours). If the lentils have absorbed all the liquid, add more as they cook. Finally, mince or chop finely and add a pinch of

6 anchovies
mixed herbs.

Stir these into the lentils and serve very hot, having cut the knuckle meat from the bone.

2　Lenticchie alla Provenzale

Soak one pound of lentils in cold
water for a few hours. Put them in a
pan with

1 onion
1 carrot
salt.

Cover well with water and bring to
the boil. Simmer until quite soft
(one and a half to two hours).
Drain them and pass through a sieve
or Mouli.

Reheat, and add

2 oz. butter
4 oz. cream.

Serve with hot boiled bacon or saddle
of hare.

3　Lenticchie alla Romagnola

Cook one pound of lentils with

twelve peeled tomatoes (or a
tin)
¼ cup olive oil
salt and pepper
2 onions, chopped very fine
2 chopped cloves garlic.

Just cover with water and bring to
the boil. Simmer, stirring constantly
and adding water when the lentils
become too dry.

Serve with roast lamb.

Lettuce/*Lattuga*

1 Lettuce salads

Wash two lettuces using the tender leaves; leave in cold water until wanted and then shake dry. Here are three dressings which go well with lettuce – but these are only three out of many.

Lettuce Dressing 1

Chop, quite finely, 2 hard-boiled egg yolks.

Beat in 1 tablespoon good olive oil.

Add salt and pepper
1 teaspoon mustard
2 tablespoons wine vinegar
3 tablespoons olive oil.

Stir well together and mix into the salad.

Lettuce Dressing 2

This is best with cos lettuce.

Mix together salt and pepper
good pinch sugar
1 dessertspoon finely chopped capers
2 tablespoons tarragon vinegar
4 tablespoons good olive oil.

Cut one good cos lettuce across into three. Wash and shake dry.

Put in a bowl with

twelve or more nasturtium flowers.

Mix in the dressing.

Lettuce Dressing 3

Wash and dry the lettuce.

Mix together

half a clove garlic, finely crushed
salt and coarsely pounded pepper.

Pour over the lettuce

a dessertspoon chopped chives.

And mix

2 tablespoons white wine vinegar
4 tablespoons olive oil.

---

2   Lattughe farcite

Wash six lettuces keeping them
whole. Plunge them in boiling salted
water until the water reboils. Drain,
refresh under cold water, and squeeze
dry.

Carefully open out the lettuces and
put in each a tablespoon of the
following stuffing:

*6 oz. minced cooked chicken
or meat
2 oz. fresh breadcrumbs
2 oz. minced chicken livers
1 egg
salt, pepper and nutmeg
pinch of mixed herbs.*

Lay the lettuces in a buttered, shallow
oven-dish (just large enough) and add

*1 glass marsala
2 oz. butter in pieces.*

Cover with a lid and bake for
twenty minutes in a moderate oven.

3 Fritto di Lattughe

Wash twelve small lettuces, keeping
them whole. Plunge them in boiling,
salted water until the water reboils.
Drain, refresh under cold water and
squeeze them dry.

Then dip them in the following
batter and deep-fry, until the root is
tender:

In a bowl put

2 heaped tablespoons flour.

Make a well; add

1 tablespoon olive oil
1 egg yolk
2 tablespoons water
salt and pepper.

Gradually mix in the flour, to a smooth
cream.

Serve, perhaps, with roast chicken.

Mushrooms/*Funghi*

Here is a list of some of the mushrooms easily found in the Tuscan hills or bought in the markets. The cèpes (*porcini*) are the most sought after and are often sliced and dried for use during the year.

Pratajnoli	(Cultivated or field mushroom)
Porcini	(Boletus edulis)
Prugnuoli	(Agaricus Georgii)
Dormienti	(Hygrophorus marzuolus)
Ovoli	(Amantia caesarea)

| **1　Funghi alla crema** | *Mushrooms and tarragon cream* |

Stew, over a good fire, with	2 lb. small mushrooms 2 sprigs chopped tarragon 4 oz. butter.
When the liquid has evaporated add	salt and pepper.
Colour the mushrooms slightly, then add – still with full fire –	½ pint thin cream.

Let it bubble until it has thickened a little, serve into little individual dishes and sprinkle with chopped parsley.

| **2　Funghi alla casalinga** | *Mushrooms in butter with anchovy, mint and lemon juice* |

Fry, in a deep frying pan, in	2 lb. mushrooms 4 oz. butter 1 tablespoon olive oil.
After five minutes, add	salt and coarsely ground pepper 4 chopped anchovies 2 sprigs chopped mint.
Mix together and then squeeze over	juice of 1½ lemons.

Fry for a moment longer, sprinkle with parsley and serve.

3 Funghi alla Francese	*Mushrooms marinated in oil and herbs, and fried*

In a casserole, put	2 lb. mushrooms.
Pickle them for one hour with	salt and pepper 2 bayleaves, chopped ¼ pint good olive oil small bunch fresh chopped mixed herbs.

Then put the casserole over a fierce fire and cook the mushrooms for ten minutes. Serve with a slice of hot ham.

4 Funghi al pomodoro	*Mushrooms cooked with garlic and tomatoes*

In a thick frying pan, fry in	2 lb. mushrooms 4 tablespoons olive oil.
After five minutes add	salt and pepper 2 cloves chopped garlic 8 tomatoes peeled, pipped and chopped.

Cook a few minutes more and sprinkle with chopped parsley.

5   Funghi all'intingolo

Mushrooms cooked with onions, parsley and white wine

In a thick frying pan, fry
in
with

2 *lb. mushrooms*
4 *oz. butter*
2 *sliced onions.*

Cook for eight minutes, then add

1 *glass white wine*
salt and pepper
plenty of chopped parsley.

6   Funghi alla pagnotta

This is a good way of cooking cèpes
or any edible funghi.

Cook the cèpes as in the previous
recipe, and meanwhile cut the top off
a small, round loaf, scoop out the
bread and fill with the mushrooms.
Replace the top slice.

Put the loaf in a roasting tray on a
bed of slices of streaky bacon and
bake in a hot oven for fifteen
minutes, basting once or twice.

7 Insalata di funghi

Slice
and marinate them in

1 lb. mushrooms
olive oil
salt and pepper
chopped parsley
3 chopped anchovies
juice of a lemon.

Serve after half an hour.

Onions/*Cipolle*

1 Cipolle al forno

Choose six medium-sized onions, and,
without peeling them, push a sprig of
fresh basil, marjoram or thyme into
the middle with the point of a small
knife. Wrap each one in foil and
bake in a moderate oven until soft.
Remove the foil and the outer skin
and serve with a little melted butter
over a sprinkling of parsley.

2 Cipolle farcite

Baked, stuffed onions

Bake six large onions in metal foil
and when soft remove the foil and
outer skin. Scoop out the centres of
the onions, which are to be chopped
with the following ingredients:

4 oz. ham (or remains of joint)
2 oz. breadcrumbs
1 oz. melted butter
2 tablespoons cream
salt, pepper and chopped
marjoram.

Mix the stuffing well, fill the onions,
place in a baking dish and sprinkle
with grated Parmesan and little pieces
of butter. Bake for a further fifteen
minutes in a hot oven.

3   Cipolle fritte

Peel and slice into rings	*4 medium onions.*

Separate them into a bowl, sprinkle milk over them and leave them for half an hour.

Drain them well and dip them in   *seasoned flour.*

Deep-fry for three or four minutes. Drain well and sprinkle with salt and pepper.

4   Cipolle glassate   *Glazed onions*

Soak in cold water for a few minutes   *1½ lb. small pickling onions.*

Peel them and put them in a frying pan with   *2 oz. butter.*

Toss them over a medium fire for ten minutes, then add   *1½ oz. sugar*
salt and pepper.

Continue cooking, without a lid, with   *½ glass port or sherry*
1 glass of water

until the onions are cooked and the liquid syrupy.

Parsnips/*Pastinace*

1 Pastinace al burro

Peel six young parsnips into a basin of cold water. Cut them in half and then into long thin batons.

Put them in a deep frying pan with

3 oz. butter
juice of a lemon
salt and pepper
1 cup water
or stock.

Bring to the boil and cook, uncovered, until the liquid is reduced and the parsnips are cooked (add more liquid if the parsnips are not quite cooked).

2 Pastinace al forno

Parboil six peeled parsnips for five minutes. Cut them into batons and put them in a frying pan with dripping. Roast them in the oven (they can be put in with a joint). When the parsnips are cooked, remove most of the fat and add a tablespoon of flour and brown on the fire. Add a cup of stock, bubble for a few minutes. Sprinkle with plenty of Parmesan and brown for ten minutes in the oven.

3   Pastinace fritte

Cut six peeled parsnips into batons
and boil them in salted water until
tender. Drain them, sprinkle with salt
and pepper, then dip them in melted
butter, and then in a mixture of half
flour, half sugar.

Heat two cups of dripping in a deep
frying pan, put in the parsnips until
they are browned on both sides.

Peas/*Piselli*

It is sad that small garden peas are nowadays very difficult to find in the shops. Usually it is the pale dry pods of the field peas, whose sweetness has become starchy, that are offered. Perhaps the good quality peas are all under contract to the big freezing companies. Home-grown peas, whether the sweet garden pea or the *petit pois* variety, are always the best. Most of these recipes, however, can easily be adapted by using frozen *petits pois* and adding other ingredients while the peas are still frozen.

1 Piselli al burro

Put a two-pint jugful of shelled peas in a saucepan with

a cup of water
4 oz. butter
salt and pepper
1 dessertspoon sugar
some parsley or mint.

Place on a hot fire. When boiling, remove the lid and stir from time to time until cooked. Remove the parsley or mint.

2 Piselli all'antica

Cook the peas as in the previous recipe, using a lettuce instead of parsley or mint. Remove the lettuce when the peas are cooked and shake in

4 oz. thick cream.

3   Piselli alla Borghese

Shell enough peas to fill a two-pint
jug and meanwhile cook gently   *1 finely chopped onion*
and   *2 chopped slices of ham*
in   *2 oz. butter*

Add the peas, a bunch of herbs, salt
and pepper and   *2 cups of good stock.*

Boil fiercely until cooked and the
liquid has reduced.

4   Piselli alla Francese

Put a two-pint jugful of shelled peas
in a saucepan with   *2 chopped lettuces*
                                        1 chopped onion, stewed in
                                        butter
                                        salt and pepper
                                        2 cups good stock.

Cook over a good heat, stirring from
time to time.

5   Piselli nel guscio   *Peas in their pods*

Remove the stalks from two pounds
of very young peas and cook them
in their pods in plenty of boiling
salted water for nearly half an hour.
Drain and serve with melted butter.

6   Sformato di piselli   *Pease-pudding*

Boil two pints of large shelled peas in
with
and

1 pint strong stock
salt and pepper
a pinch of all-spice.

When cooked, pass the peas through
a fine sieve and return to a low flame,
adding

2 oz. butter
1 tablespoon flour
3 yolks of eggs
2 crushed macaroons.

Heat through, stirring well, remove
from the fire and cool slightly while
you beat

3 egg whites.

Fold them in and put the mixture in
a buttered soufflé dish. Cook in a
container of hot water in a moderate
oven for half an hour.

Polenta/Maize flour

Maize flour is not much used now, even in Italy, where Northerners are sometimes called *polentoni* by the Southerners. The most successful use for maize flour is in making bread, when it would be mixed with wheat flour; two thirds maize flour to one third wheat flour. It is a bread that goes well with a meal, particularly a simple meal of salami and cheese.

1   Polenta alla Parmigiana

Into
stir, a little at a time,

1 pint boiling salted water
1 lb. Indian cornflour.

Boil until smooth, then turn out into an oiled tray, spreading out the mixture until it is half an inch thick.

When cool cut it into inch pieces and pile in layers in a baking dish, interspersed, liberally, with melted butter and grated Parmesan, finishing with butter and Parmesan. Bake in a medium oven for forty minutes.

2   Polenta con salcicce

Polenta with garlic sausage or zampone

Make the polenta as in the last recipe and cool on a tray. While it is cooking, boil some garlic sausage – or the rich Italian *zampone* – for half an hour.

Skin and dice the sausage, mix it with some tomato purée and a little stock. Pile alternate layers of polenta and sausage in a baking dish with grated Parmesan and pieces of butter between each layer. Sprinkle finally with Parmesan and butter and bake in the oven for half an hour.

Serve very hot with a crisp salad with a slightly sweetened dressing.

Potatoes/*Patate*

1   **Patate alla Borghese**   *Potatoes with butter and lemon*

Boil two pounds of potatoes in their
skins (or two pounds of new potatoes
scraped). Drain and peel them and
cut in thick slices into a shallow
oven-proof dish.

Add

4 oz. butter
chopped parsley
salt and pepper.

Simmer with a lid and add   *the juice of 2 lemons.*

Serve hot.

2   **Patate alla campagnuola**   *Sliced potatoes with nutmeg and cream*

Boil two pounds of potatoes in their
skins, drain, peel and slice them thin.

Heat them in a thick frying pan with

4 oz. butter
salt and pepper
nutmeg.

Colour slightly, then add   *¼ pint cream.*

Shake thoroughly and serve hot.

3 Patate in casseruola

A ring of mashed potatoes with a centre of tomato pulp

Peel and chop	*8 good-sized ripe tomatoes.*
Put them in a pan with	*juice of ¼ an onion* *2 tablespoons olive oil* *salt and pepper.*
Cook slowly while you prepare the potatoes.	
Mix in a saucepan, over a low fire,	*1 lb. mashed potato* *4 egg yolks* *¼ pint cream* *2 oz. butter.*
Stir frequently until the potatoes form a paste, then season with and arrange in spoonfuls round a dish.	*salt and pepper*
Pour the tomato into the centre of the ring and sprinkle with grated Parmesan.	

4   Patate alla crema

Boil twelve potatoes in their skins.
Drain, peel and chop them.

In a pan, put

4 oz. butter
½ onion, chopped
chopped parsley
chopped mint
salt and pepper.

Stew with a lid on until the onion is
cooked. Then remove the lid, mix
in the potatoes and

1 cup single cream.

Shake well until the mixture boils.
Sprinkle with parsley and serve.

5 Crocchette di patate

Boil eight potatoes. Drain well and
leave the pan on the side of the stove
for a minute to dry out the potatoes.

Put them through a sieve or Mouli
and put the purée in the saucepan
with:

2 egg yolks
a little grated onion
juice of a lemon
chopped parsley
2 oz. butter
2 tablespoons of cream
a pinch of cinnamon and
grated nutmeg.
salt and pepper.

Mix the purée with these ingredients
thoroughly with a wooden spoon on
a low fire until the mixture stiffens.
When cool, roll into little sausages on
a floured board. Egg and breadcrumb
and fry in hot fat until golden.

6   Patate al forno

Bake six large potatoes. When
cooked, cut them in two and remove
the insides with a spoon. Mash the
scooped-out potato with a fork and
add

4 oz. butter
½ pint hot milk
salt and pepper
6 crushed juniper berries.

Mix well together and add

2 beaten egg whites.

Fill the skins with the paste and fork
over the top.

Cook in a hot oven until crisp and
golden.

7   Gnocchi di patate

Boil eight potatoes. Drain well and
leave to dry for a minute on the side
of the stove. Pass through a sieve or
Mouli, return the purée to the
saucepan and add:

2 oz. grated Parmesan
2 oz. flour
3 eggs
salt, pepper and nutmeg.

Mix well and cool.

Make into little rolls on a floured
board. Put them – a dozen at a time –
into boiling salted water (do not boil
fiercely) for a few minutes until they
rise and are firm. Place on a dish in a
cool oven until they are all done, then
pour over melted butter and sprinkle
with grated Parmesan.

8   Patate all'Italiana

Wash and peel off a strip round eight
potatoes. Boil in salted water for
twenty minutes until cooked. Drain
them well and sieve them. Put them
back in the pan with

2 oz. butter
4 slices crustless bread, soaked
in milk
½ cup milk
3 egg yolks
salt, pepper and nutmeg.

Mix well together and add

3 beaten egg whites.

Pile high in a baking dish, sprinkle
with melted butter and grated
Parmesan and bake until golden for
fifteen to twenty minutes.

9   Budino di patate con funghi

Boil eight potatoes. Meanwhile,
quarter and fry in butter

1 lb. open mushrooms.

Add

salt and crushed peppercorns
2 tablespoons cream.

Shake the pan and reserve until the
potato purée is made.

Drain and sieve the potatoes. Add

2 oz. butter
¼ cup cream
3 egg yolks
salt and good pinch pepper.

Butter a soufflé dish and put the
purée in the bottom and sides, leaving
a well in the middle and some purée
to put on top. Put the cooked
mushrooms in the middle and seal
with the rest of the purée. Cook for
twenty minutes in the oven and turn
out on to a dish (but leave in the
soufflé dish if the potato has stuck
to it).

Note. This potato purée can have a
variety of fillings – leeks, spinach,
small broad beans, all mixed with a
little cream.

10 Patate arrostite

Scrape three pounds of new, equal-
sized round new potatoes.

Heat *4 oz. butter*
and *2 tablespoons olive oil*
in a large deep frying pan and
add *the potatoes, salt and pepper.*

Cover with a lid, place on a fairly
low fire and shake frequently. They
will take a good half hour and should
have a good brown crust.

11 Patate in stufato

Cut six large peeled potatoes into
approximately quarter-inch cubes.
Put them in a baking dish just
covered with milk. Sprinkle with
2 oz. butter, cover and bring to the
boil, then put in a hot oven until
tender (still with the lid on).

12   Patate Tartufate

Potatoes cooked with truffles and Parmesan

Slice four large potatoes fairly thin and wash them in cold water. Lay them in a buttered baking dish with layers of potato, sliced Piedmontese white truffles (if you can get them) and grated Parmesan cheese. Finish with grated Parmesan, sprinkle with butter and lemon juice and moisten with good chicken broth (about half way up the baking dish). Bake in a fairly hot oven until tender (about forty minutes).

13   Insalata di patate con vino e acciughe

Potato salad with wine and anchovies

Mix six finely sliced cooked potatoes with

1 bunch spring onions, chopped
1 glass red wine
salt and crushed pepper
1 cup olive oil
½ tablespoon wine vinegar
chopped chervil and parsley
twelve roughly chopped anchovies.

Mix together and leave to marinate before serving.

14 Insalata di patate   *Potato salad*

Slice six cooked potatoes. Slice 3
hard boiled eggs and mince 6 oz.
tunny fish. Place alternate layers of
potato, egg and minced tunny fish.
Pour over a vinaigrette in which
there is chopped fresh fennel.

Pumpkin/*Zucca*

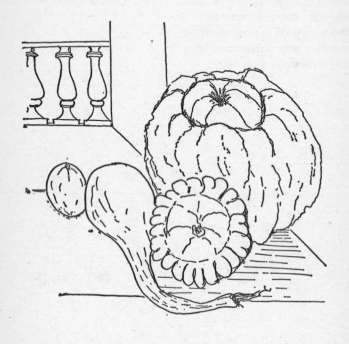

1 Zucche ripiene

Small pumpkins filled with tunny fish and spice, served with tomato sauce

Cut in half either three small American squashes (the size of your fist) or six large courgettes – about six inches long.

Scoop out the insides with a dessertspoon, throwing away the seeds but preserving the pulp.

Mix the pulp with

3 egg yolks
an 8-oz. tin of tunny fish with the oil
1 tablespoon grated Parmesan
pinch of all-spice and pepper
small pinch salt.

Fill the half pumpkin shells with the mixture. Sprinkle with more grated Parmesan and bake in a moderate oven with a lid.

Serve with a tomato *coulis*, made simply by sweating
in

½ finely chopped onion
olive oil.

When cooked, pour in
and

1 tin Italian tomatoes
salt and pepper.

Stew for twenty minutes and serve.

2   **Zucche fritte**
Strips of pumpkin or marrow fried in olive oil

Peel, halve and seed six courgettes (about six inches long) or one small pumpkin (smaller than a football). Cut the flesh into strips, the size of chips, and leave them in a sieve sprinkled with salt for a couple of hours (to get rid of excess moisture).

Heat olive oil (or frying oil) in deep pan. Dip the strips in seasoned flour and fry until cooked and light brown.

Drain well and serve at once, with a squeeze of lemon.

3   **Zucche alla Fiorentina**

Boil three small American squashes in salted water. When soft, drain, cut in half and remove the seeds.

In the middle put

cream
a small knob of butter
salt, pepper and nutmeg
squeeze of lemon.

Bake in a hot oven for ten minutes.

Sprinkle with chopped chives and serve.

Sorrel Purée/*Puré di acetosa*

The most practical way of using sorrel is to make it into a buttery purée which will keep in a glass jar in the refrigerator. This can then be used for a soup, a fish sauce, an omelette, mixed in with some young cooked peas, or with chopped cooked potatoes and cream.

Wash the sorrel carefully and put it into a pan with a little boiling water, season lightly and cover. Uncover and stir now and again until the sorrel is soft and a brownish colour (only three to four minutes). Drain and mix with melted butter. Keep in the refrigerator until needed.

Spinach/*Spinaci*

1 Spinaci al burro

Remove the stalks and wash two
pounds of spinach in a sink full of
cold water. Drain the spinach and
shred it.

In an earthenware pot put 2 oz.
butter and when this has melted add
the spinach, salt and pepper and a lid.
Stir constantly until the spinach is
cooked. If the spinach appears too wet
when almost cooked, remove the lid
and finish cooking until the juices
have evaporated.

2 Spinaci alla crema

Remove the stalks and wash two
pounds of spinach in a sink full of
cold water. Drain and chop it.

Melt 2 oz. butter in an earthenware
pot, and add the spinach, salt and
pepper. Cover with a lid removing
it to stir the spinach constantly. When
the spinach is cooked remove it from
the pan and let the juices bubble.

Stir in 1 dessertspoon ($\frac{1}{2}$ oz.) flour and
$\frac{1}{4}$ pint cream, stir until it bubbles
and thickens, add the spinach and a
little grated nutmeg and 3 hard-boiled
eggs, roughly chopped. Reheat
thoroughly and serve.

3 Crocchette di spinaci

Remove the stalks and wash two pounds of spinach in a sink full of cold water. Drain well, chop and put in an earthenware pot with salt and pepper. Stir frequently and cover with a lid. When cooked, drain it and press dry. Chop it again and replace it in the earthenware pot with

4 oz. butter
a small bunch of marjoram, chopped
1 teaspoon of sugar
a little grated zest of lemon.

Mix well over the fire and put in

¼ pint milk.

When it boils add

2 beaten-up eggs.

Remove from the fire and stir until the egg thickens. Allow to cool. Then roll into small sausages.

Meanwhile make the batter:

Mix

1 tablespoon olive oil
¼ glass white wine (or water)
salt

into

2 oz. flour.

Roll the croquettes in this batter and deep-fry.

Serve with sections of lemon.

4 Ravioli alla Fiorentina

Remove the stalks and wash two pounds of spinach. Drain and cook in boiling salted water. When the water reboils, drain the spinach. Run cold water over it and press it very dry with the hands. Chop finely and put in a saucepan with

1 oz. flour
2 oz. butter
8 oz. fresh curd cheese
(Ricotta)
3 egg yolks
salt, pepper and nutmeg
2 oz. grated Parmesan.

Stir briskly for a minute or two and allow to cool. When cold roll into small pointed sausages (an inch long). Flour them and lower them into boiling salted water. Simmer and as they rise remove them from the fire. Pour over melted butter, sprinkle with grated Parmesan and serve.

5 Spinaci in riccioli

Remove the stalks and wash one pound of spinach, boil in salted water for a few minutes, drain well. Rub it through a sieve (alternatively use frozen chopped spinach). Beat up 2 eggs with salt and pepper and mix in the spinach.

Pour a little olive oil into an omelette- or pancake-pan, heat thoroughly and pour in a little of the mixture as for making a pancake, i.e. as thin as possible. Turn it over, take it out and repeat until all the mixture is used, stacking the pancakes on top of one another.

Shred the pancakes into fingers and pour over them a purée of tomatoes (simply tomatoes and seasoning sweated in oil with a lid on and then passed through a sieve).
Sprinkle with Parmesan. Brown in a hot oven.

Good with smoked sausages, or the pancakes can be shredded into consommé.

6   Sformato di spinaci   *Spinach soufflé*

Wash, cook and sieve	*2 lb. spinach.*
Heat in a saucepan then add and cook	*1¼ oz. butter* *1½ oz. flour.*
Add and bring to the boil	*¼ pint thin cream.*
Season with	*salt, pepper and nutmeg.*
Mix in without boiling	*2 egg yolks.*
When cool, whisk and fold in	*3 egg whites.*

Half fill individual soufflé dishes. Sprinkle well with Parmesan and bake in a moderate to hot oven for ten to fifteen minutes, depending on the size of the dishes.

Serve, needless to say, at once.

Note. If this is cooked for a party, prepare the soufflé base ahead with all but the egg whites in it. The base should be warm but not hot or cold. Whip and fold in the egg whites so that the soufflé will be cooked when you wish to eat.

7 Sformato di spinaci con funghi

Either make a purée of spinach (as in *spinaci in riccioli*) or heat two half-pound packets of frozen spinach purée in

2 oz. butter.

Cook until fairly dry. Add the juice of

½ a lemon.

Leave to cool. Beat up with

3 egg yolks
one whole egg.

Butter a mould – preferably a ring mould, or, if not, a soufflé dish. Add the spinach to the egg and the mixture to the mould. Cook *au bain marie* for an hour in a moderate oven and when set, turn out and pour mushrooms fried with a little garlic and finished with tomatoes and seasoning into the middle.

Tomatoes/*Pomodori*

1 Conserva di pomodori — *Tomato conserve*

Wash as many ripe or nearly ripe
(not over-ripe) tomatoes as you wish.
Put them in a deep saucepan, sprinkle
with salt and pepper and sugar, put
on a lid and cook slowly, stirring
from time to time until the tomatoes
are a pulp.

Pass the pulp through a Mouli or
sieve. Preserve in jars or keep it in a
refrigerator with olive oil on top; or,
in these days of large deep-freezes,
pour the cold purée into polythene
bags and freeze until needed.

This purée is a basic ingredient to
much of Italian cooking. It is used in
soups, risottos, sauces and many meat
dishes.

2   Pomodori alla griglia alla senape

Grilled tomatoes with a mustard dressing

Halve six large ripe tomatoes without skinning them and put them to grill, cut side up, with salt, pepper and a brushing of olive oil.

While they are grilling baste with a dressing of

1 tablespoon olive oil
juice of ½ a lemon
small teaspoon sugar
small teaspoon French mustard
little salt and pepper.

Place the tomatoes in a hot dish with the dressing. Sprinkle with parsley.

3   Pomodori al forno

Cut six large ripe tomatoes in half without skinning them. Scoop out some of the pips and centre with a teaspoon. Prepare a stuffing with sweated in

six sliced mushrooms
1 tablespoon olive oil
chopped small clove of garlic
pinch of chopped parsley
pinch of chopped chives.

Fill the tomatoes with the stuffing and sprinkle with Parmesan.

Bake for ten to fifteen minutes.

4 Pomodori alla panna

Scald and peel twelve small ripe
tomatoes.

Heat in an earthenware pan   *1 tablespoon olive oil.*
Sweat without colouring   *1 chopped onion*
and add   *1 tablespoon chopped fresh*
                               marjoram
                               ½ oz. flour.

Cook for a minute and add   *salt and pepper*
                               ¼ pint thin cream.

Bring the cream to the boil, shaking
the pan occasionally. Add the
tomatoes and cook on top of the stove
or in a very hot oven for five minutes
or until the tomatoes are cooked.
Serve sprinkled with chopped
parsley.

5 Pomodori con uova

Take six large tomatoes, cut off the
top and keep it aside to make a lid.
Scoop out the middle carefully and
break an egg into each tomato.
Season with salt and pepper and a
little chopped tarragon, add a nut of
butter and replace the tomato lid.
Place the tomatoes on a well buttered
dish and season them lightly. Bake in
a very hot oven until the eggs are set
(10–12 minutes).

The tomatoes can be served on a
round base of buttered toast covered
with a slice of ham.

Other tomato stuffings:

1) left-over risotto.
*2) chopped anchovies, olives,
garlic and breadcrumbs.*
*3) chopped mushrooms and
shrimps.*
*4) flaked cooked smoked
haddock – serve with garlic
mayonnaise.*

6 Gelatina di pomodori   *Tomato jelly*

Heat one pint of tomato preserve.

Add

> *1 tablespoon finely chopped chives*
> *juice of a lemon to taste*
> *pinch of cayenne.*

Pour over

> *one ½ oz. packet of dissolved gelatine*

and pour into a ring mould.

Turn out when set and fill the centre with fresh prawns mixed with a little mayonnaise.

7 Insalata di pomodori

Tomato salads

(a) Slice six tomatoes (peeled first or not, according to your wish) and dress with

1 tablespoon tarragon vinegar
2 tablespoons good olive oil
sprinkling of sugar and salt
chopped chives.

(b) Scald and peel six tomatoes. Halve them and scoop out the seeds (keep them for a soup or stew). Fill the tomatoes with chopped hard-boiled egg mixed with mayonnaise and chopped tarragon.

(c) Slice the tomatoes. Chop some celery very finely and sprinkle over them. Pour over some vinaigrette dressing.

(d) Slice the tomatoes and make a lattice-work over them with thin strips of anchovy. Roughly chop some stoned black olives and sprinkle over. Pour over a little vinaigrette dressing to which has been added a little crushed garlic.

(e) Choose large tomatoes, peel them (if preferred) and slice them lengthways. Alternate the slices of tomatoes with slices of peeled Italian peach, overlapping well. Season with salt and pepper, sprinkle lemon juice over and a little walnut oil.

Mixed Vegetables and Salads

1   Sformato di verdura

Flan of vegetables; baked vegetable cake

Use a total of of which there should be	3 lb. mixed vegetables 1 lb. potatoes.
Prepare them and cut them up fairly small. Put them in a saucepan with	2 oz. melted butter 1 cup water salt and pepper 1 bunch sweet herbs.
Cover with a lid and stew gently until cooked. Then add	1 cup cream.
Stir and leave to cool.	
Mix in and fold in	4 yolks of eggs 4 oz. grated cheese 4 beaten egg whites.

Put the mixture in a buttered mould,
well lined with breadcrumbs,
cover with more breadcrumbs and a
buttered paper and bake in a
moderate oven for forty minutes.

2 Verdure miste brasate

Mixed braised vegetables (a winter dish)

Prepare the following vegetables, cutting the carrots, turnips and leeks into three-inch strips:

$\frac{1}{4}$ *lb. small onions*
$\frac{1}{2}$ *lb. carrots*
$\frac{1}{4}$ *lb. turnips*
$\frac{1}{2}$ *lb. leeks*
$\frac{1}{2}$ *lb. celery*
1 *medium cabbage.*

Arrange the onions, carrots, turnips and leeks in a large shallow oven-dish. Almost cover with and add

stock
salt and pepper
pinch of mixed herbs.

Braise in a moderate oven for half an hour.

Meanwhile, blanch the cabbage for five minutes in boiling salted water. Drain and cut into six pieces, each with a little stalk; arrange the cabbage with the other vegetables. Cook for a further twenty minutes.

Sprinkle with plenty of parsley. Take care that the vegetables are not over-cooked, for the flavour will lose freshness and become 'gassy'.

3   Cappon magro

A mixture of spring vegetables, piled up into a pyramid.
Serve with a plain roast

This mixture can vary a good deal, but this list will indicate some of the range of choice. Use at least six of them:

small new potatoes
small onions
baby carrots
small French beans
courgettes
bulb fennel
small sliced artichokes
broad beans
asparagus
cauliflower
small peas
tomatoes.

The only rule to follow is that the root vegetables should be cooked separately, starting with cold water. The others are cooked in boiling water.

The vegetables, when cooked and drained, are mixed together and tossed in melted butter and more salt and pepper.

4   Fritto misto   *Mixed fried vegetables*

Traditionally, this is a dish of fried
vegetables with fried calves' brains
and chicken rissoles. The following
recipe, however, omits the meat.

Prepare the following vegetables:

Pare, cut into slices and keep in cold
water   *6 young artichokes.*

Top and tail and cut into long ¼-inch
strips   *4 small courgettes.*

Quarter and take out the seeds of   *3 red peppers.*

Blanch for five minutes and separate
into flowers   *1 small cauliflower.*

Finally, with the following
stuffing fill   *twelve courgette flowers.*

Clean, cook and squeeze dry   *1 lb. spinach*
and mix in   *3 demi-sel cheeses*
                                                      1 egg
                                                      salt, pepper and nutmeg.

Fry all these vegetables, in stages, in
deep fat, first dipping them in the
following batter:

Put in a bowl   *4 oz. flour*
                                                      salt and pepper.

Make a well; put in   *2 egg yolks*
                                                      3 tablespoons olive oil.

Start mixing in the flour and gradually add	½ pint water
until it is smooth and like thick cream.	
Finally, add	2 beaten egg whites.

Mixed Salads/*Insalate miste*

1 alla Cardinale

Wash a lettuce and a bunch of
watercress.

Cut into strips	*3 small beetroot.*
Quarter	*3 hard-boiled eggs.*
Wash	*12 radishes.*
Slice	*½ cucumber.*

Arrange them all on a shallow dish
and serve with a creamy mayonnaise:

Put in a bowl	*2 egg yolks.*
Very gradually add and	*¼ pint olive oil 1 dessertspoon white wine vinegar.*
Add	*salt and pepper 2 tablespoons cream.*

2 all'Italiana

Cook
and

1 lb. new potatoes in their skins
¼ lb. baby carrots.

Peel the potatoes. When cold, cut
the potatoes and carrots into slices.

Then cut
into two-inch lengths, then in half and
then shred very finely.

2 washed leeks

Mix the vegetables together with the
following Sauce Lombarda:

In a bowl, put
and add, very gradually,

2 egg yolks
¼ pint olive oil
salt and pepper
1 dessertspoon lemon juice
1 dessertspoon tomato purée
1 dessertspoon chopped fresh
herbs.

3 alla Macedone

Mix together

> ½ lb. cooked French beans
> ½ lb. cooked young peas
> ¼ lb. soaked and cooked
> haricot beans.

Dress with the following vinaigrette –
the olive oil should be the finest:

> 2 tablespoons wine vinegar
> salt and pepper
> 1 tablespoon chopped chives
> 4 tablespoons olive oil.

4 alla pollastra

Arrange on a dish the following:

> 2 sliced peppers
> 6 tomatoes, quartered
> the remains of a cold chicken
> 1 small cos lettuce, shredded
> 24 stoned olives.

Make a vinaigrette sauce with salt,
pepper, sugar, vinegar and olive oil,
and add a little cream. Pour over the
salad.

5 **alla Russa**	*Mixed salad with prawns, capers, anchovies and mock caviare dressing*

Cut up and mix together cooked	*asparagus* *French beans* *peas* *young carrots.*
Add	*some capers* *anchovies* *prawns.*
Pour over a sauce made with	*salt and cayenne pepper* *1 teaspoon mustard* *½ grated onion* *small jar Danish 'caviare'* *3 tablespoons vinegar* *6 tablespoons olive oil.*

Rice/*Riso*

Cooking Rice

Wash the rice and pour it into plenty of boiling salted water. Stir the rice until the water reboils, and continue boiling for about a quarter of an hour, until the rice is just soft between the teeth. Drain it in a colander and rinse briefly under hot water, serve or put in a buttered casserole, cover with a lid and keep hot – but not too hot.

Pilafs and Risottos

The basic difference between a pilaf and a risotto is firstly the amount of liquid in which the fried rice is cooked. Pilaf should be dry and have the

same quantity of liquid as of rice; a risotto should be moist and needs half as much liquid again as a pilaf. Secondly, whereas a pilaf is a plain, flavoured rice dish (say with saffron or herbs), usually served as an accompaniment, a risotto has a high proportion of additional ingredients, making it a dish in itself. The commonest mistake with a risotto is to have too high a proportion of rice.

The rice in pilafs and risottos should be fried first in the best olive oil obtainable. Pilafs and risottos should 'repose' for a few minutes once they are cooked. The rice during this time absorbs more moisture.

1 Pilaf

In an earthenware pot fry
in

½ finely chopped onion
2 tablespoons good olive oil.

Add and fry
then add

8 oz. rice
1¼ pint stock or water and
bouillon cube
1 bayleaf
salt and pepper if necessary.

Bring to the boil, cover and simmer
gently on top of the stove or in a
moderate oven for nearly half an
hour, until the rice is cooked. Remove
this from the stove and leave without
a lid in a warm place or oven for a
few minutes and serve.

2 Riso alla Ristori

In an earthenware casserole put

4 oz. green bacon, chopped
1 chopped onion
¼ to ½ shredded white cabbage
a little salt, pepper and sugar
6 slices garlic sausage,
quartered.

Cover with a lid and stew for half an hour; add

4 oz. Italian or Patna rice
¾ pint stock .
1 tablespoon chopped parsley.

Simmer gently for a further twenty minutes and serve with grated Parmesan.

3 Riso al pomodoro

In an earthenware casserole put

2 tablespoons olive oil
1 finely chopped onion
1 chopped clove garlic

and stew without colouring.

Add and fry

8 oz. Italian rice.

Add

1 tablespoon chopped marjoram
1 pint tomato pulp (see p. 147)
salt and pepper.

Bring to the boil, simmer for about
twenty minutes, until the rice is
almost cooked, remove from the fire
and leave to rest for five minutes
before serving with grated Parmesan.

---

4   **Risotto ai funghi secchi**   *Rice with dried cèpes*

In a small bowl soak in warm water	*2 oz. dried cèpes.*
In an earthenware casserole heat	*2 tablespoons olive oil.*
Add and fry without colouring	*1 finely chopped onion* *1 good clove of garlic, chopped.*
Add and fry	*6 oz. Avorio rice.*
Add the soaked and chopped	*cèpes* *pinch of thyme* *1 pint stock or water and* *chicken bouillon cube* *mill-ground pepper.*

Bring to the boil, and simmer gently
for twenty to twenty-five minutes.
Leave to rest for five minutes and
sprinkle with parsley and cheese.

Risotto ai gamberi	*Risotto with prawns*
In an earthenware casserole put	2 tablespoons olive oil.
Add and fry without colouring	1 finely chopped onion 1 chopped clove garlic.
Then add and fry and	6 oz. Italian rice 12 good-sized Mediterranean prawns in their shells.
Add	1 level dessertspoon of tomato purée juice of a lemon pinch of mixed herbs pinch of cayenne 1 pint water with chicken bouillon cube.

Bring to the boil and simmer in a moderate oven with a lid for nearly twenty minutes, until the rice is just soft to the bite. Put the risotto to one side to 'repose'; correct the seasoning and serve.

6 Riso pilaf allo zafferano *Saffron pilaf*

In an earthenware casserole put	*2 tablespoons olive oil.*
Add and fry without colouring	*1 finely chopped onion.*
Add	*8 oz. Italian or Patna rice* *½ coffee-spoon crushed saffron.*
Fry the rice and add	*1 pint stock* *juice of one lemon.*

Bring to the boil, cover with a lid, and simmer in the oven or on top of the stove for about twenty minutes, until the rice is really cooked. Take off the heat and leave it to stand for five minutes.

7 **Risotto alla Poggio Gherardo**	*Risotto with marsala and chicken livers*

In an earthenware casserole heat	*2 tablespoons olive oil.*
Add and fry	*1 chopped onion* *6 oz. rice.*
Then add	*1 port-glass marsala.*
Let it bubble almost dry and add	*1 pint chicken stock* *small pinch of mixed herbs* *good pinch crushed pepper.*
Then add	*4 chopped chicken livers* *(roughly 4 oz.).*

Simmer for twenty minutes.
Let the rice rest for five minutes and
serve with grated Parmesan.

8   Risotto alla Milanese

In an earthenware casserole heat	*2 tablespoons olive oil* *1 oz. butter.*
In this, fry till golden	*1 chopped onion.*
Add	*6 oz. sliced mushrooms* *a large pinch crushed saffron* *1 chopped truffle (optional).*
Stir in and fry	*6 oz. Avorio rice.*
Add	*1 pint chicken stock* *1½ oz. grated Parmesan.*

Simmer for eighteen minutes. Let it
rest and serve with grated Parmesan.

9 Crocchette di riso e spinaci   *For using cooked rice*

Mix together

8 tablespoons cooked rice
1 lb. cooked spinach squeezed
dry and chopped
2 eggs
ground nutmeg
salt and pepper
1 oz. grated Parmesan
grated rind of one lemon.

Bind, if too soft, with a little flour.
Then with floured hands roll into
sausages on a floured board and dip
in beaten egg and breadcrumbs and
fry golden.

Macaroni/*Pasta asciutta*

Making *pasta* is not difficult nor does it take too long, but space in the form of a good-sized kitchen table is essential for rolling out the paste as thin as paper. In Italy there always seem to be a few black-clad grandmothers and aunts who have the build for kneading and the time to spare.

The commercial pasta, however, is fairly good – except for perhaps with *lasagne* and *ravioli* where the fresh pasta is noticeably better. Some fifty varieties are presented in the catalogues of pasta manufacturers; tubes, shells, rods, nuts and bolts, the whole display having the appearance of an ironmonger's advertisement.

The commercial *lasagne* needs blanching for ten to fifteen minutes, unlike the home-made, which only needs five minutes in boiling salted water. The *fettucini* and macaroni to be served simply with butter and cheese or with a sauce will need a little more than fifteen minutes, depending on its shape and size. When cooked, it should be *al dente* – with a slight bite to it. Someone I know hurls a strand of spaghetti at the wall and if it sticks, it is cooked.

To make Pasta

In a basin put	*1 lb. plain flour.*
Make a well and break in	*3 eggs.*
Add	*1 scant teaspoon salt.*
Break up the eggs with a wooden spoon and gradually incorporate the flour. Gradually add about	*4 fluid oz. water.*

Then knead until elastic (about five minutes). Divide the paste and roll out paper-thin until just about transparent, dusting lightly and frequently with flour. Leave to rest for half an hour and then cut as required into oblongs for *lasagne* and *cannelloni*; small squares for ravioli; or rolled and shredded for *tagliatelle*.

1 Fettucine alla crema

'Ribbons' served with cheese and cream

Stick an onion with a clove and cook it with one pound of *fettucini* or *tagliatelle* in boiling salted water for nearly twenty minutes. When just cooked, drain well and remove the onion.

Return to the saucepan with

2 oz. butter
4 oz. grated Emmenthal
2 oz. grated Parmesan
a little grated nutmeg
6 fluid oz. cream.

Cook for a few minutes over a low flame until the cheese melts and becomes elastic. Serve very hot.

2 **Maccheroni al forno**

Lasagne *baked with mozzarella cheese*

Blanch one pound of *lasagne* in boiling salted water or stock for fifteen minutes until just soft. Meanwhile, slice two *mozzarella* cheeses thinly (these can be bought in Soho). Drain the pasta when cooked and refresh under running hot water. In a thick baking dish alternate the pasta with layers of cheese, seasoned with ground pepper, nutmeg and grated Parmesan. Finish with pasta, sprinkle with grated Parmesan, breadcrumbs and a few small nuts of butter, bake in a hot oven until brown and sizzling. (Beware, the *mozzarella* will be extremely elastic.)

3 Spaghetti alla Napoletana

A sauce of mushrooms,
(white truffles), tongue and
tomatoes

Cook one pound of spaghetti for
nearly twenty minutes until just soft.
Drain it well and return it to the
saucepan and pour over the following
sauce:

In a small saucepan heat

1 tablespoon olive oil.

Add and fry without colouring

1 small chopped onion.

Add and cook

¼ lb. chopped mushrooms.

Then add

1 small tin of tomatoes, crushed
salt and pepper
a little chopped white truffle
2 oz. chopped tongue.

Simmer gently for five minutes,
serve very hot and also with grated
Parmesan.

4   Spaghetti alla Quaresima

Spaghetti with parsley, anchovies and white wine

Boil one pound of spaghetti in salted water for about twenty minutes until just soft. Drain well and serve with the following sauce:

Heat in a small saucepan

1 tablespoon olive oil.

In it, fry golden

1 large chopped onion
1 clove chopped garlic
8 chopped anchovies
1 glass white wine.

Reduce the wine and add

8 fluid oz. fish stock (from a turbot or cod's head) or water.

Season with

a pinch of white pepper
2 tablespoons chopped parsley.

Serve this sauce with the spaghetti and a bowl of grated Parmesan. Flaked fish, prawns, mussels or squid can be added to the sauce.

5 Maccheroni alla Siciliana

Lasagne *cooked with chopped cooked veal, ham, eggs and herbs*

Blanch three quarters of a pound of *lasagne* for fifteen minutes until nearly soft, drain and refresh under hot running water.

Meanwhile chop

1 lb. cooked veal (beef or lamb will do)
4 oz. ham.

Slice
and chop

4 hard-boiled eggs
2 tablespoons marjoram, chives, little basil and chervil.

Butter a baking dish (a fairly shallow casserole). Lay pieces of *pasta* on the bottom, then meat, eggs, herbs and seasoning, more *pasta*, another layer of meat etc., and finally a layer of *pasta*.

Pour in enough

stock or water with chicken bouillon

nearly to cover.

Sprinkle with grated Parmesan and a few small nuts of butter and bake in a hot oven for twenty minutes until browned.

6   Timballo ai funghi

Cooked fettucini *coiled inside a mould filled with* fettucini *and mushroom sauce; then baked*

Cook one pound of *fettucini* in boiling salted water until nearly soft. Drain and allow to cool. Butter a timbale mould or pudding basin (about seven inches in diameter).

Meanwhile prepare the following sauce:

Melt in a frying pan and add

2 oz. butter
1 chopped clove garlic
8 oz. sliced button mushrooms.

Cook until the moisture of the mushrooms has evaporated and add

1 oz. flour.

Mix in and add

½ pint good stock
1 tablespoon chopped marjoram salt and pepper.

Simmer for ten minutes.

Coil some of the cool *fettucini* round the inside of the timbale well packed and slightly overlapping until the sides and base are covered. Mix the sauce with the remainder of the *fettucini* and pour into the middle of the mould. Put the mould in a baking dish of water, cover the

mould with a saucer and place in a
moderate oven for forty minutes.

Turn out carefully on to a hot dish
and serve with grated Parmesan and a
fresh purée of tomatoes (twelve
tomatoes squashed into a saucepan,
seasoned, covered and stewed for ten
minutes and then passed through the
Mouli).

7   Pappardelle con lepre

Wide noodles with hare sauce

Cook some wide strip noodles (wider than *fettucini*) in boiling salted water until nearly soft (about twenty minutes), drain and mix with the following sauce, made from legs and shoulder of hare. (Use the saddle of hare for roasting.)

In a thick frying pan heat	*1 tablespoon olive oil.*
Add	*4 oz. streaky bacon, chopped* *½ chopped onion* *1 clove garlic, chopped* *1 chopped piece of celery.*
When brown add the small pieces of rolled in	*chopped hare* *seasoned flour.*
Brown the hare and add	*1 glass red wine* *1 glass stock.*
Season with	*thyme* *salt and pepper.*

Cover the pan and cook slowly for an hour.

Shake the sauce; pour into a bowl and serve with the noodles.

8 Agnolotti alla Poggio Gherardo

Home-made ravioli *with minced chicken, (truffle), butter and cream*

Mince finely, twice

1½ lb. cooked chicken.

Sweat
in

½ chopped onion
4 oz. butter.

Stir butter and onion into the chicken and add

salt and pepper
pinch of tarragon
1 chopped white truffle
(optional)
1 sherry glass of dry white vermouth
4 fluid oz. cream (single).

Work the mixture to a paste.

Make a pound of *pasta* (see p. 172), divide it and roll it paper-thin. Leave it to rest for half an hour and then put teaspoonfuls of the chicken mixture on one piece of *pasta* at about two-inch distances, brush very lightly in between with egg-wash and lay the second sheet of *pasta* lightly on top. Press down round the little heaps and then cut out with a knife or one of those small scooped wheels.

Have ready a large saucepan of boiling salted water and put in it the *ravioli*. Boil slowly for about eight minutes. Take them out with a strainer; season with melted butter and Parmesan cheese. Serve very hot.

9 Crescioni

Little pasta *turnovers filled with spinach, herbs and cream and deep-fried*

Wash and boil

1½ *lb. spinach.*

Drain well, pressing the spinach dry with the back of a wooden spoon. Roughly chop the spinach and put it in a frying pan with

3 tablespoons very good olive oil
2 small cloves garlic, chopped
grated nutmeg
salt and pepper
1 tablespoon fresh chopped herbs such as marjoram, chervil and chives
2 tablespoons grated Parmesan.

Mix the spinach and the ingredients, simmer for five minutes, remove from the stove and leave to cool.

Meanwhile make *pasta* as described on p. 172 and roll it out thin as paper. Leave it to rest for half an hour and cut into three-inch squares. (Thinly rolled puff pastry will also do quite well.) Put a little heap of spinach on one square at a time and fold over like a turnover, brushing the edges with egg-wash. Seal the edges firmly and when they are all prepared, deep-fry them for three minutes on each side in not too hot oil until lightly coloured. Dust with grated Parmesan

and serve on a napkin with a fresh
purée of tomatoes (twelve ripe
tomatoes squashed into a saucepan,
seasoned, covered and stewed for ten
minutes and then passed through
the Mouli).

10 Tagliatelle alla Romagnola

Thin strip noodles fettucini, with garlic, tomatoes and small garlic sausages

Cook a pound of *fettucini* or home-made *pasta*, cut into strips, in boiling salted water until just soft (fifteen to twenty minutes). Meanwhile make the following sauce with sausages:

In a thick frying pan heat

3 tablespoons olive oil.

In it fry gently

3 cloves garlic, chopped parsley twelve small fresh garlic sausages or good butcher's sausages.

When the sausages are nearly cooked add

1 tin tomatoes (14–16 oz.) salt and pepper to taste.

Let the sauce and sausages stew for ten minutes.

Drain the *fettucini* and lay in a dish, making a well in the middle. Arrange the sausages and sauce in the middle and sprinkle with grated Parmesan. Serve very hot.

Almost all the soups in this book have a basic form of onion and potato, further vegetable and stock added later. Potato, I find, is a better thickening for soup than flour, partly because it is a vegetable itself and not a cereal and also because the consistency is fresher and more palatable. Today the use of electric blenders, which save much time and labour, has revived the serving of delicious home-made soups.

Minestra di asparagi   *Asparagus soup*

It would be extravagant to use bunches of asparagus just for soup unless you have a garden with weak roots that are too thin to eat as a vegetable or can buy the sprue asparagus from the shops. Ideal, however, is to use the trimmings from asparagus when they are to be prepared as a vegetable, those white chalky ends.

Cut off, then, the thick white stalks of the asparagus (about one third of the length) and wash them. (Boil the green parts as recommended on p. 8, but reserve a few tips for garnishing the soup.)
Alternatively use two pounds of sprue, reserve and boil the very tips, and use the rest for the soup.

In a thick-based saucepan, melt   *2 oz. butter.*

Add

1 small onion, chopped
3 medium potatoes, peeled
and sliced

and the

asparagus trimmings or sprue.

Season slightly with
and cover with a lid.

salt and pepper

Sweat for fifteen minutes, remove
the lid and add

2 pints milk.

Stir and add a small bunch of

parsley.

Bring to the boil and simmer for
fifteen minutes. Pass through a fine
Mouli or sieve. Return to a saucepan,
bring to the boil, correct the
seasoning and the consistency with a
little cream and garnish with tops of
asparagus. Serve with fried croûtons.

2 Minestra di cavolo e maiale   *Cabbage and pork soup*

This, like with many soups, is open to different combinations, but be careful with this soup (as, indeed, with any other vegetable soup) that it is not over-cooked, for the flavour becomes stale.

Remove the stalk from	*½ small white cabbage or ¼ large one.*
Cut the cabbage in two or three slices and shred it finely.	
Finely chop	*½ lb. piece salt streaky or mild streaky bacon.*
Put it in a saucepan with	*1 tablespoon dripping or butter.*
Lightly fry the bacon with	*1 shredded onion.*
Add the and	*shredded cabbage freshly milled pepper.*
Stir the cabbage over the fire for a few minutes and then add	*2 pints stock or water.*
Bring to the boil and simmer for twenty minutes. Skim from time to time. A few minutes before serving correct the seasoning and add and/or a few	*1 finely sliced cooking apple crushed chestnuts.*

3   Minestra di carote

Carrot soup

In a thick pan (with a lid) melt and add

2 oz. butter
1 roughly chopped onion
4 large peeled and chopped carrots
1 small peeled and chopped turnip
12 crushed coriander seeds.

Season lightly with

salt and pepper.

Cover with a lid and heat gently for twenty minutes, then add

2 pints stock or water and chicken bouillon.

Bring to the boil and simmer for twelve minutes. Pass the soup through a medium-mesh Mouli or strainer, return to the saucepan and reboil. Correct the seasoning and consistency with a little more stock and finish with

½ cup chopped herbs (a combination of chives, parsley, chervil, marjoram, thyme or rosemary).

Serve with fried croûtons.

4 Minestra di cetriolo alla crema *Cucumber and cream soup*

Peel strips of skin from and liquidize with

1 cucumber
1 large or 2 small dill pickled cucumbers
juice of a lemon
½ onion, grated.

After liquidizing stir in

6 fluid oz. cream
salt and pepper
1 tablespoon chopped dill.

If necessary add a squeeze of lemon juice. Keep chilled and serve with a little diced cucumber in the soup.

5 Minestra di lenti   *Lentil soup*

It is important to have a good chicken
or meat stock for this soup.

Soak
for a few hours in warm water.

½ lb. brown lentils

Put the soaked lentils into a saucepan
with

1 onion, roughly chopped
1 chopped stick of celery
1 carrot, finely chopped
4 pints good stock.

Bring to the boil and simmer for an
hour to an hour and a half, until the
lentils are soft. The stock will have
reduced by about a pint. Skim, and
season with the following mixture:

In a bowl mix

6 finely chopped anchovies
1 chopped clove of garlic
2 tablespoons chopped parsley
6 leaves sage, chopped
4 fluid oz. good olive oil
12 roughly crushed peppercorns.

Stir this mixture well into the soup;
remove from the fire and allow to
rest (the lentils will absorb some of
the oil). Reheat before serving and
mix well.

Minestra di lattuga   *Lettuce soup*

good summer soup hot or cold, but
served cold reduce the amount
f potato. Use lettuces that remain
nderdeveloped in the garden, the
aves of ones that have just bolted or
e outside leaves of about three
ttuces.

a saucepan melt
nd add

2 oz. butter
1 medium-sized onion,
chopped
3 medium peeled and diced
potatoes.

over with a lid and stew gently for
wenty minutes.

emove the lid and add

2 pints chicken stock or water
and chicken bouillon.

ring to the boil and add the

roughly chopped lettuce
leaves
a small bunch of chervil
pepper and salt (if necessary).

oil for ten minutes and then pass
hrough the fine Mouli. Return to
he saucepan and before serving add

6 oz. cream (thin)
chopped chives and chervil.

7   **Minestra di piselli**   *Pea soup*

An easy soup to make, using the pods
and the peas, but a good Mouli is
essential.

In a saucepan put

> *3 lb. peas in their pods,
> roughly crushed
> 1 grated onion
> small bunch sweet herbs.*

Add

> *3 pints boiling water
> salt and pepper.*

Bring to the boil and boil uncovered
for half an hour. Boil fiercely to keep
the colour of the peas. Pass the soup
through a coarse Mouli and then
through the fine. Return to the
saucepan and reboil for five minutes.

Correct the seasoning, add
and serve with fried bread croûtons.

> *3 tablespoons thick cream*

Minestra di zucca

*Pumpkin soup
(a spiced soup)*

Peel and roughly dice a

2 lb. slice of yellow pumpkin.

Put it in a saucepan with

*2 oz. butter
1 chopped onion
12 coriander seeds
large pinch cumin
salt and ground pepper
1 medium potato, peeled and
chopped.*

Cover with a lid and simmer for
twenty minutes. Remove the lid, add

*3 pints stock or water and
chicken bouillon.*

Bring to the boil and simmer for
thirty minutes, uncovered. Pass the
soup through the coarse disc of the
Mouli, return to the pan and reboil.
Check the seasoning and add fresh
milled pepper, a small spoonful of
cream for each bowl, and chopped
parsley.

9 Cream of onion soup

In a saucepan melt	*2 oz. butter.*
Peel and chop and put them in the saucepan with	*5 medium-sized onions* *3 peeled and diced potatoes* *(medium-sized)* *salt, pepper and nutmeg.*
Cover with a lid and stew gently for twenty minutes. Add and bring to the boil.	*2 pints chicken stock*
Boil for ten minutes and pass through a fine Mouli. Return to the saucepan and add	*½ pint single cream.*
Correct the seasoning and garnish with chopped parsley and fried bread croûtons.	

10 Minestra di carciofi di Giudea

Jerusalem artichoke soup

Peel and slice into a bowl of cold water (with a piece of lemon)

6 good-sized Jerusalem artichokes.

Peel and chop

1 onion.

In a saucepan melt

2 oz. butter.

Add the onion and Jerusalem artichokes and season lightly with

salt and pepper.

Cover with a lid and simmer gently for ten minutes.

Remove the lid and add

2 pints of milk.

Bring to the boil. Simmer gently for a further ten minutes and pass the soup through the fine Mouli. Return the soup to the saucepan. Reboil and correct the seasoning, add a little

single cream
chopped chervil

and fried bread croûtons, before serving.

11 Polentina alla Veneziana   *Maize-flour soup*

Bring to the boil and skim	*3 pints good chicken broth.*
Mix into a little of the stock	*3 tablespoons polenta (fine maize flour).*

Stir to a paste.

Stir the paste carefully into the stock, then gradually add	*3 oz. butter.*

Serve with fried bread croûtons.

12 Minestra di acetosa   *Sorrel soup*

In a saucepan melt and add	*2 oz. butter* *2 peeled and chopped onions* *3 peeled and chopped potatoes.*
Season with	*salt and pepper.*
Cover with a lid, simmer gently for twenty minutes. Remove the lid and add	*3 pints chicken stock* *$\frac{1}{2}$ lb. washed sorrel.*

Bring to the boil and simmer for five minutes. Pass through a coarse Mouli and serve with croûtons and a little cream added to each bowl of soup.

13   Minestra di crescione   *Watercress soup*

In a saucepan melt   *2 oz. butter*
and add   *1 onion, peeled and chopped*
                                                3 medium-sized potatoes
and the stalks of   *3 bunches watercress.*

Cover with a lid, season with   .   *salt and pepper*
and stew gently for twenty minutes.

Remove the lid and add   *2 pints chicken stock*
and the remainder of the watercress.

Bring to the boil and cook for ten
minutes, pass through the medium
Mouli and return to the saucepan
and add   .   *½ pint single cream.*

Correct the seasoning and consistency.
Garnish with chopped parsley.

14 **Minestra di spinaci**   *Spinach soup*

Into
put

and

3 pints chicken stock
2 medium-sized potatoes,
peeled and sliced
1 bunch chopped spring onions.

Bring to the boil and cook for
twenty minutes and add

1 lb. spinach, washed and
roughly chopped

and a little grated nutmeg. Cook for
a further ten minutes. Pass through a
coarse Mouli and season. Finish with
a little cream cheese softened with
cream.

15 Minestra di pomodori   *Tomato soup*

In a saucepan melt
and add

2 oz. butter
1 onion, peeled and chopped
1 medium-sized potato,
peeled and chopped.

Cover with a lid and simmer gently
for twenty minutes.

Remove the lid and add

3 lb. ripe tomatoes
1 pint chicken stock
(or to make a quick soup – 1
large tin Italian peeled
tomatoes).

Bring to the boil and simmer for ten
minutes, pass through a medium
Mouli and return to the saucepan.
Re-season, adding a pinch of sugar,
and garnish with a little chopped
basil, marjoram or parsley.

| 16 **Minestra di verdura, erbe e crema** | *Vegetable, herb and cream soup* |

Into a saucepan melt
and add

> 2 oz. butter
> 2 chopped sticks celery
> 1 chopped leek
> 1 chopped carrot.

Season with salt and pepper,
cover with a lid and stew gently for
twenty minutes. Add

> 3 pints chicken stock
> 1 roughly chopped lettuce
> ¼ lb. sorrel or spinach, washed
> and chopped.

Bring to the boil and simmer for ten
minutes. Pass through the medium
Mouli and return to the saucepan.
Reboil, correct the seasoning and add

> 3 tablespoons chopped herbs
> (which might include chervil,
> chives, marjoram and a little
> thyme or tarragon).

Add a little cream before serving.

More about Penguins and Pelicans

Penguinews, which appears every month, contains details of all the new books issued by Penguins as they are published. From time to time it is supplemented by *Penguins in Print*, which is our complete list of almost 5,000 titles.

A specimen copy of *Penguinews* will be sent to you free on request. Please write to Dept EP, Penguin Books Ltd, Harmondsworth, Middlesex, for your copy.

In the U.S.A.: For a complete list of books available from Penguins in the United States write to Dept CS, Penguin Books, 625 Madison Avenue, New York, New York 10022.

In Canada: For a complete list of books available from Penguins in Canada write to Penguin Books Canada Ltd, 2801 John Street, Markham, Ontario L3R 1B4.

Mediterranean Food

Elizabeth David

This book is based on a collection of recipes made by the author when she lived in France, Italy, the Greek Islands, and Egypt, doing her own cooking and obtaining her information at first hand. In these pages will be found recipes, and practical ones, evoking all the colour and sun of the Mediterranean; dishes with such exciting and unfamiliar names as the *Soupe au Pistou*, the *Pebronata* of Corsica, or the *Skordaliá* of the Greeks. The book includes recipes from Spain, Provence, Greece, Italy, and the Middle East, making use of ingredients from all over the Mediterranean now available in England. The majority of the dishes however do not require exotic ingredients, being made with everyday vegetables, herbs, fish, and poultry, but treated in unfamiliar ways.

'In *Mediterranean Food* Mrs David proves herself a gastronome of rare integrity . . . She refuses to make ignoble compromises with expediency. And in this, surely, she is very right . . . Above all, she has the happy knack of giving just as much detail as the average cook finds desirable; she presumes neither on our knowledge nor our ignorance' – Elizabeth Nicholas in the *Sunday Times*

a Penguin Handbook

French Provincial Cooking

Elizabeth David

Elizabeth David always succeeds in inducing a desire to use each recipe as soon as it is read. Whether she is describing the preparation of a plain green salad, or the marinading of a haunch of wild boar, she writes with the same imaginative directness. Recipes like *pot au feu* are described in all their delicious simplicity, which, it is made clear, means cooking without elaboration and has nothing to do with the higgledy piggledy 'let's hope it's all right' technique. Some excellent advice is included on the choice of the tools that would always be needed in any kitchen.

'It is difficult to think of any home that can do without Elizabeth David's *French Provincial Cooking* . . . One could cook for a lifetime on the book alone' – *Observer*

'If I had my way I would have a copy purchased by public funds and presented to every young wife on her wedding day' – Vivian Rowe in *The Traveller in France*

'Make a beeline for Elizabeth David's new comprehensive study . . . this book will add a new depth of authority to your knowledge' – *Queen*

French Country Cooking

Elizabeth David

In this book Elizabeth David, author of *A Book of Mediterranean Food*, describes some of the splendid regional cookery of France. The food of every region has its own particular flavour, derived naturally from the local resources; in *French Country Cooking* will be found a large variety of recipes, from the primitive peasant soup of the Basque country to the refined Burgundian dish of hare with a cream sauce and chestnut purée. There is also a chapter on the use of wine in the kitchen and advice as to suitable cooking utensils.

'I love this book. It is forthright, highly imaginative and intensely practical. It is just what the discriminating have been looking for' – Ambrose Heath in *Queen*

'A remarkable book ... here, indeed, is another world from ours. It knows nothing of the ready-packaged product, the five-second whip-up; here food is treated with reverence, with understanding and, above all, with care' – Elizabeth Nicholas in the *Sunday Times*

a Penguin Handbook

ENGLISH COOKING, ANCIENT AND MODERN I

Spices, Salt and Aromatics in the English Kitchen

Elizabeth David

In this volume, the first in an original study of English cooking, Elizabeth David presents English recipes which are notable for their employment of spices, salt and aromatics. As usual, she seasons instruction with information, explaining the origins and uses of such ingredients as nutmeg, cardamon and juniper. Mrs David stresses the influence of centuries of oriental trade on the English kitchen, where spices and Indian curry, kebabs and yoghurt are now perfectly at home, along with immigrant dishes such as rissotto, paella and pepper steak.

This book, with its brawns (or pig's-head cheese), briskets and spiced beef, its smoked fish and cured pork, its old-fashioned curd dishes and sweet fruit pickles, sounds a welcome, if uncommon, note in the English kitchen.

'Has all the characteristic qualities of her earlier books. There is that same precise evocation of how food should look and smell and the same lack of pretentiousness, the same scholarly approach, combined with forthright opinions and suggestions' – Lucia van der Post in the *Sunday Times*

The Best of Eliza Acton

Edited by Elizabeth Ray with an introduction by

Elizabeth David

Eliza Acton's famous *Modern Cookery for Private Families* was first published in 1845 and remained in print for over seventy years. Although in taste and spirit a product of the eighteenth century – the dishes described would have been familiar fare on the tables of Lord Byron, Jane Austen and Tobias Smollett – its appeal has successfully survived the test of time.

In this new edition Elizabeth Ray has carefully selected recipes from the original with an eye to what is manageable in twentieth-century kitchens. And, while giving the recipes exactly as they were written by Miss Acton (whose style is not the least charm of this classic book), she has added notes and explanations about terms and equipment to help the modern cook.

'The young women of today', writes Elizabeth David in her introduction, '. . . will bless Miss Acton for her clarity, for her positive attitude and for the memorable comments and instructions which bejewel her pages.'

Italian Food

Elizabeth David

Exploding once and for all the myth that Italians live
entirely on minestrone, spaghetti, and veal escalopes, this
exciting book demonstrates the enormous and colourful
variety of Italy's regional cooking. Listing well over four
hundred dishes, clearly described and helpfully classified,
the author of *A Book of Mediterranean Food* and *French
Country Cooking* also enumerates the various herbs and
spices required in many of them, sensibly explaining where
they may be bought, and there are useful chapters on
Italian wines and cheeses. The result is an extremely
readable guide to eating out in Italy which is also a practical
text-book for reproducing the best of Italian food in your
own kitchen.

'I do not remember any other cookery book which has so
impressed me' – Margaret Lane in the *New Statesman*

'Certainly the best book we know dealing not only with
the food but with the wines of Italy' – *Wine and Food*

'It is the great book on Italian cooking in English'
– *Hugh Jonson*